A Pictorial Guide to Worcestershire

Eight Walks in
South Worcestershire

A Pictorial Guide to

Worcestershire

Book One: The Southern
Half of the County-
Worcester to Broadway

Carl Flint FRSA

Malvern Walks

Eight Walks in South Worcestershire
A Pictorial Guide to Worcestershire
Book One: The Southern Half of the County–
Worcester to Broadway
Carl Flint

Published by Malvern Walks, 2021
Barnards Green Road, Malvern, Worcs. WR14 3NB

2 4 6 8 10 9 7 5 3 1

Designed, printed and bound by Aspect Design
89 Newtown Road, Malvern, Worcs. WR14 1PD
United Kingdom
Tel: 01684 561567
E-mail: allan@aspect-design.net
Website: www.aspect-design.net

ISBN 978-0-956629548

EIGHT WALKS IN

SOUTH WORCESTERSHIRE

This book is dedicated to my family and friends who
have supported my writing endeavours.

Contents

Acknowledgements

Over the years since I first undertook the enjoyable task of researching and writing 'The Pictorial Guide' series my children have grown from toddlers to adults. During their teenage years there was not a 'cat in hells chance' they would join dad for a walk in the countryside. As they moved towards and into their twenties there has been a slight perceptible change. Possibly due to the Duke of Edinburgh scheme, walking is now OK again. Although saying that Josh Flint has accompanied me on a number of occasions with a suitable bribe of a pint of real ale at the end of the walk. Josh has also helped with the technical stuff like getting the Malvern Walks website up and running, linking Facebook to the website and helping to install software. I bought him a drone so he could film me on the walks, but such has been the backlash from protestors flying drones over Heathrow Airport, aerial shots may well not feature much in my YouTube walks productions!

Justine Sissons has proofread every book with the exception of the first edition of book one. There were so many mistakes that friends and I missed, a proper proof reader had to be found and Justine, thank goodness, came to my rescue.

Additionally, following the local Alfrick and Lusley show a number of years ago where to the surprise of my family and friends my home-made wine was awarded first prize, I bumped into Colin Soley whose children had attended the same primary school as mine. Following that encounter we often meet up for a chat and a few beers and this led to him joining me on quite a number of walks that are featured in these three volumes.

Author's Note

The 'Wainwright style' of the text and pictures is of course intentional. I have used it for my first five Pictorial Guides (even the name is borrowed from him). I don't believe anyone has surpassed the incredible detail he included in his drawings and the dry sense of humour of his documented walks. If the documentary I saw about his life was accurate he would take photographs of his walk and have the black and white film developed and produce his wonderful drawings from his photographs. This is what I do (in a digital environment), but alas my drawing skills are not up to his standard. There are however a few of my drawings in the first Pictorial Guide, but they took me far too long to produce and did not quite 'cut the mustard'. So, using my position of power as Vice Principal at Worcester College of Technology (as it was called then) I set the HND Computing students a task to find a software programme that would create line drawings from photographs. They came up with Akvis which is a stand-alone package which can be tried for free for a month and caters for professional and non-professional user licences—at very little cost, I may add.

Getting There

As mentioned in the following introduction Worcestershire is a county often passed through but not often visited, but hopefully this guide will help the county become more of a 'destination' than it currently is. Even less visited is Herefordshire to the west which on reflection if what I hear from the locals is true, they are very happy to keep it that way! The Wye Valley is just so stunningly beautiful and it is one of my favourite destinations for a day out. To the north-west, Shropshire, Leominster, Ludlow and the Long Mynd provide very attractive walkers destinations. To the north-east the Birmingham conurbations are held at bay by the Lickey and Clent Hills. Directly east is Warwickshire with its Shakespeare inspired Stratford Upon Avon and to the south Gloucestershire.

Recently the M5 has undergone lane widening works in an attempt to alleviate the congestion around the M6 and M42 junctions. However, during the morning and evening rush hours the traffic is still very heavy and best avoided if possible. By the time this book is published the Carrington Bridge over the River Severn will be undergoing lane widening activity, so complete chaos will be in place for many months if attempting to reach Malvern via the Worcester ring road.

The 'A' roads in Worcestershire outside of the rush

hour are really not that bad but do expect to be held up by old people in Malvern and tractors just about anywhere, especially during the harvest period. The road to Hereford has just got to be the most diabolical for accidents caused by frustration at slow moving farm traffic. So please take care, we have banned our offspring from driving along this road!

All of the walks in this book have public transport links. Actually, this is not quite true as Sundays are mostly bereft of buses. Steam train fans might like to indulge themselves with a train journey from Cheltenham Racecourse to Broadway on the Gloucestershire Warwickshire Steam Railway.

Introduction to South Worcestershire

Worcestershire is a small diverse land-locked county. In a car you can travel its length within half an hour along the M5 and if the minor roads are clear east to west it is just under the hour. Although millions of folk pass through Worcestershire en-route for the West Country or head north to Manchester, Liverpool or North Wales it is not generally a well-known county. I can verify this statement as my first visit to Worcestershire was not until 2001 at the tender age of forty-three!

Ask folk what they know about Worcestershire. The historians will mention that King John is buried in Worcester Cathedral and that the English Civil War began and ended in Worcester. Music scholars will recount Edward Elgar's Enigma Variations inspired by his connections with Malvern and the Last Night of the Proms favourite, The Pomp and Circumstance March. Motor sports fans will identify the last bastion of British car production in the UK with The Morgan Motor Company. Literary academics will identify the influence of Malvern on J. R. R. Tolkien, C. S. Lewis and George Bernard Shaw. If we start digging a little deeper into the history of Worcestershire, pub quiz experts will recall that Huddington Court a fifteenth-century moated manor house was the family home of the Gunpowder Plot conspirators Robert and Thomas Wintour and is close to the village of Crowle. Nikolaus

Pevsner described it as 'the most picturesque house in Worcestershire'. Capability Brown had his first commission at Croome Park. The water cure which placed Malvern on the map is not so well known out of the county and since Schweppes stopped selling Malvern Water in 2010 long gone are the sophisticated advertising hoardings at many international airports which gave one a sense of 'pride of place' when travelling abroad. Dyson Perrins of Lea and Perrins Worcestershire Sauce fame lived in Malvern.

During the Victorian era Malvern became famous amongst the landed gentry for its water cure and many luminaries such as Florence Nightingale and Charles Darwin visited Great Malvern to try a cure for their ailments.

The Vale of Evesham in the south-east of Worcestershire is well known for its production of fresh produce in the form of bags of salad which is shipped to supermarkets all over the UK. More traditional crops such as the springtime asparagus and plums from Pershore in the autumn are well known by 'foodies' and horticulturists alike. Britain's longest river, the Severn splits the county east-west and is often in the news because of severe flooding along its reaches in Bewdley, Worcester, Upton and just to the south of the county, Tewkesbury in Gloucestershire.

In relation to popular culture, fans of the Archers will know that the legendary Bull Inn is based in the delightful village of Inkberrow to the east of Worcester on the Stratford road. Nigel Mansell who won the Formula 1 World Championship in 1992 was born in Upton upon Severn and attended Worcester College of Technology. Food writer, journalist and broadcaster

4

Nigel Slater also attended Worcester College of Technology. Rick Stein attended a prep school in Malvern and Jeremy Paxman attended Malvern College. Toyah Willcox, the 1980s singer, I was delighted to find out whilst researching for this book was the voice of the Tellytubbies and lives in the centre of Pershore in a rather fine Georgian house.

It is said that Worcestershire has over four miles of footpaths for every square mile of its surface making it one of the most accessible counties in the UK. For keen walkers a number of long-distance footpaths cross the county provide an excellent opportunity to explore further afield such as the Worcestershire Way, The Three Choirs Way, the Severn Way, the Monarch's Way, Heart of England Way, Millennium Way, North Worcestershire Path, the Wychavon Way, Cotswold Way and Shakespeare's Avon Way.

For lovers of hill walking The Malvern Hills are probably the most well-known, however the very southern tip of the County dips into the delightful picturesque Cotswolds. Bredon Hill bordering the eastern side of the Severn valley overlooks Pershore and Eckington. To the north of the county the Lickey and Clent Hills provide stunning views into Shropshire and across Birmingham.

South Worcestershire Map

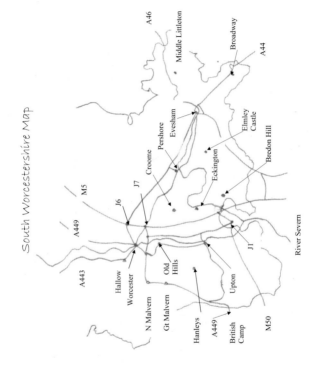

How This Book is Organised

I learnt from writing the Malvern Pictorial Guides that attempting to cover the whole area in one go was fated to be out of date by the time it was published, so for this reason the county of Worcestershire has been split north to south. Volume one is the south, because its nearer to home. Volume two covers the north of the county and volume three will provide a further eight walks across the county.

Each walk described is circular and so could theoretically be started at any point. As you may have already picked up liquid refreshment stops are a great source of pleasure, however, do bear in mind the frequency of hostelries closing down appears to be accelerating and so best to 'Google' the establishments before leaving. Every attempt has been made to include public transport options where they exist.

The Waypoint listing at the end of each walk provides an extra level of information for those with GPS devices or those particularly skilled at map reading. The description preceding the Waypoint may seem a little obscure but it is a direct copy from the text. So, 'Old stone wall SO 97993 39887' aligns to the particular section of the walk text.

References to Other Supporting Materials to Enhance the Walks

The Ordnance Survey Landranger map 150 Worcester, The Malverns & Surrounding Area does a pretty good job in covering most of the county. However, the Explorer Maps provide the required depth to enjoy most of the nooks and crannies. To cover the southern half of the county the following maps will need to be purchased:

190 Malvern Hills & Bredon Hill

OL45 The Cotswolds

204 Worcester & Droitwich Spa

205 Stratford-Upon-Avon & Evesham

A Brief Resume of South Worcestershire's History

Worcestershire has such a fascinating topographical and historical diversity which surely identifies it as the county which most encapsulates all that is England. South Worcestershire is dominated on three sides by hills. The Malverns to the west, Bredon to the east and the Cotswolds to the south. The major towns in the south of the county are Worcester, Malvern, Pershore and Evesham.

Firstly Worcester, it is known that the Romans occupied Worcester due to the importance of the River Severn for trading and access to the west. In 680 missionaries from Northumbria founded the cathedral. At the end of the tenth century the Bishop of Worcester, Oswald started to construct a new cathedral, however in the early eleventh century the Danes under King Cnut and his son Harthacnut sacked the monastery. The locals turned on Harthacnut's henchmen and murdered them. It is said that their skins were then nailed to the cathedral door. In response Harthacnut destroyed both the city and cathedral. Towards the end of the eleventh century Wulstan a much respected and politically astute Bishop had the cathedral rebuilt. Wulstan became a Saint when he was buried in the cathedral. It is believed that King John had a special devotion to St Wulstan and wished to be buried in Worcester Cathedral.

King John's son Henry III grant of a charter in 1227

established the Guildhall. Originally a substantial wooden structure it was rebuilt in the Queen Anne style in 1772 by the stone mason, Thomas White, a student of Sir Christopher Wren. Above the main doors is a magnificent gilded coat of arms of the Hanoverian dynasty. The interior is equally impressive with a grand Italianate styled Assembly Room. An interesting painting of Queen Victoria painted by James Saint is well worth seeing as it was not re-painted in black mourning attire following Prince Albert's death.

Not far away in New Street is Greyfriars a black and white timbered merchant's house which was rescued from demolition. It was originally thought this was the remains of a Franciscan Friary but assessment by English Heritage concluded that this was a late medieval merchant's house dating to around 1489.

No trip around Worcester can ignore the importance the city played during the English Civil War. In 1642 The Battle of Powick is cited by many local text books, but appears in the wider context to be more of a skirmish when King Charles I's treasure train containing valuables from the Oxford Colleges and elsewhere was on its way to the Kings mint at Shrewsbury and was intercepted by Prince Rupert. However, The Battle of Worcester in 1651 was a full-blooded affair with up to five thousand Parliamentarians and Royalists killed.

Worcester was once well known for glove manufacturing with leather skins arriving by river from Bristol and lamb's skins from Derbyshire. In 2011, there was an article in the Worcester Evening News, describing Les Winfield aged ninety-one as one of the two remaining workers from Worcestershire's last French Seam glove factory based near Lower

Broadheath. The spire of the former St Andrews church located in Deansway is known locally as the Glover's Needle, probably the only physical reminder of this once thriving industry.

The Quakers were not only highly influential in developing the glove industry but also in 1751 setting up Worcester Porcelain. The company had a Royal Warrant from 1788 and was known as Royal Worcester. On my arrival in Worcester in 2001 as Vice Principal of the Technical College the company was in terminal decline with redundancies up to 2006 when finally it went into administration. The Portmeirion Group acquired the brand name and intellectual property rights in 2009.

Cricket fans will of course describe the New Road cricket ground close to the banks of the River Severn with its tree-lined stunning backdrop of the cathedral as one of the most attractive grounds in the country. It has been home of the Worcestershire County Cricket Club since 1896.

Heading south the name 'Malvern' comes from the Welsh 'Moel Bryn' meaning Baldhill. In 1924 excavations identified that the hills were used as beacons as far back as the Iron Age to produce smoke by day and flames by night, for communicating religious festivals, trade movements and acts of war. The modern town owes its origins to the arrival of the Benedictine monks in the early 1080s, who during the last part of William the Conqueror's reign established Malvern Priory.

William Langland the author of the epic 'Piers Plowman' poem was educated at Malvern Priory. The poem describes life in England during the fourteenth century and it is regarded as the greatest Middle English poem prior to Chaucer.

In 1745 Dr. John Wall, one of the founders of Worcester Porcelain published his analysis of Malvern water and described the purity of the water to be outstanding. The town continued to expand, and in 1842 Doctors Wilson and Gully came to Malvern and set-up their respective hydropathic enterprises. With the expansion of the rail network to Great Malvern in 1862, this greatly improved accessibility to this popular spa town appealing to tens of thousands of visitors to Malvern each year. It is therefore not surprising that many eminent figures of the Victorian era found themselves attracted to Malvern. These include Charles Darwin, Florence Nightingale, Charles Dickens, Alfred Lord Tennyson and Peter Roget to name but a few.

To date, Malvern spring water continues to be sold throughout the world. It is allegedly the only bottled water Her Royal Highness Queen Elizabeth II will drink. The Malvern's inspired Elgar's music, Tolkien's misty mountains and C. S. Lewis with the gas lamp to the entrance to Narnia.

To the south-east the delightful market town of Pershore can trace its history to 681 when King Ethelred gave land for the foundation of a religious house. Until the Dissolution of the Monasteries the town of Pershore had been part-owned and governed by Westminster Abbey. During the English Civil War Pershore commanded a strategic river-crossing point and in 1644 King Charles' army demolished an arch of the bridge after escaping from Oxford.

In the eighteenth century the town was formerly on the main London to Worcester road and thus became an important staging post for the horse drawn coaches. Today the impressive Angel Inn and Post House opposite the old marketplace in Broad Street is a good reminder of how busy Pershore must have been.

The development of Pershore as a market town is in part due to the abundance of local fertile land and its ability to grow a considerable range of fruits and vegetables. Nowadays, the most well-known crop is the Pershore Plum. The story goes that in 1833 the landlord of the Butcher's Arms George Crooks discovered in the nearby Tiddesley Woods the Egg Plum. Orchards were soon grown to exploit this crop and in 1890 a cross between plums produced the now famous Pershore Purple.

Pershore's agricultural heritage continues to this day with Pershore College of Horticulture, now known as Pershore College. It is a national centre for horticulture and is situated on a sixty-hectare site just past the two bridges on the Evesham Road.

The Vale of Evesham stretches from the Cotswold Hills on the south and east and is bordered by Bredon Hill on the south-west. Rich soil deposits of alluvial loam and the shelter of the surrounding hills provides England's finest market garden. Although the Vale of Evesham was extensively occupied by the Romans there is little evidence that they set up residence in Evesham. In 709 Evesham was known as Eveshomme and by 1086 took on the current form. The town is located on a horseshoe peninsula formed by a loop of the River Avon and is almost completely surrounded by water. The town is susceptible to heavy flooding documented back to the thirteenth century. More recently 1998 and 2007 saw two of the heaviest floods ever recorded.

Evesham Abbey was founded by Saint Egwin the third Bishop of Worcester in around 701. Henry VIII's Dissolution of the Monasteries in 1540 saw the abbey dismantled leaving only the Lichfield Bell Tower standing.

The Battle of Evesham in 1265 was the second of two main battles of the Second Barons War. Prince Edward, son of Henry III who led an eight-thousand-strong army massacred Simon de Montfort's army who were cornered at the end of the horseshoe bend in the river. It is believed that the St George's flag was used for the first time at this battle.

Near the Abbey Gate is the Almonry Museum and Heritage Centre housed in a fourteenth-century half-timbered building formerly the home of the almoner (a monk who was in charge of providing alms to the poor) of Evesham Abbey.

A popular entertainment centre attracting folk to Evesham is the classical Art Deco styled Regal Cinema which reopened in 2009. In addition to music, stand-up comedy and of course cinema all seated in comfy chairs, sofas and a bar makes this venue a pleasant evening out.

Walking Gear

What should you take when embarking on these walks? Bear in mind none of them classify as long-distance walks and are never far from a hostelry or refreshment stop. However, a decent pair of walking boots particularly in the winter months is essential. Mine are my long-serving Mendle walking boots which may not be always spotlessly clean but are packed in the car along with thick walking socks. Gaiters are absolutely invaluable in winter or when wet. You can walk into your house after a walk without fear of lumps of dirt falling off all over the place. Especially in winter I take my Graghoppers Solar dry lightweight walking trousers, otherwise whatever feels comfortable given the temperature and precipitation. Talking of which, I was undertaking a walk near Ledbury for Rob Stewart who runs a PR/media company that specialises in mountains and ski destinations and also equipment. One of his clients Linda from Maier Sports was none to impressed with my old 'Graggies' and asked for my vital statistics whereupon, a few weeks later, a pair of super lightweight, state of the art Maier Sports walking trousers arrived by post. Such is the power of the media!

From my experience of jogging all-year round, layers of long-sleeved tops are essential and, of course, short-sleeve versions in high summer. Clothes with deep pockets helps to ensure stuff is not lost en route.

Suitable headwear is often forgotten about. I have a beanie for cold weather and a peaked cap for sunny days. I have two rucksacks, the largest is twenty litres but I prefer to take the smaller one if possible. All it holds clothes wise is an extra top layer and rain-proof top. My Karrimoor has got to be over twenty-five years old and is still going strong!

This guide should be more than adequate to enable the walk to be completed successfully, however the relevant map as listed previously will enhance the experience.

I am not a hot tea flask or stewed coffee man so it's either water or a small carton of fruit juice, a muesli bar and often a sandwich is all I take on a walk as enjoying a refreshment stop or two and reflecting on the walk is such a satisfying experience. Everyone nowadays has a mobile phone often complete with mapping and satellite tracking so communication in an emergency should not be a problem.

Health and Safety

Ever heard of risk management? It's all about planning what might and could happen and what effect it would have on you. An example of poor risk management is when I forget the suntan lotion and then suffered a burnt face with a considerably increased risk of skin cancer. However, I have learnt to take enough clothes a change of clothes in the car if its chucking it down with rain. Regarding the planning element if the forecast is awful, I don't go on the walk!

Four factors which can upset the 'apple cart' is fog, animals, construction work, and flooding. The first time I walked up to Broadway Tower I could not see its massive structure until I was just fifty metres away such was the fog. Springtime in particular can be troublesome when crossing a field with young cattle. They are naturally inquisitive beasts when young and are certainly not aware that their quarter of a ton multiplied by the number in the herd heading towards you at some considerable speed would cause you serious hurt or worse. The blocked route due to construction work of some description is not that common but can throw things off course. Rivers in flood in wintertime are more likely to cause problems especially in Worcestershire so plan ahead.

The Walks

Walk One
Broadway Village to the Tower

Summary

The county of Worcestershire is fortunate to dip its toe into the Cotswolds ensuring that the large village of Broadway with its honey coloured Cotswold stone is quite unique. The traditional built Cotswold stone houses and cottages dominate this 'film set' of a picturesque English shire village. There are, as you would expect with this tourist honey pot, an abundance of charming shops and restaurants to enjoy.

Broadway Hill rises steeply from the village to the second-highest point in the Cotswolds. Where positioned on a dramatic outlook stands Broadway Tower, a four-storey folly inspired by Capability Brown.

Heading out of the village this reasonably strenuous

4.2 mile/6.7km walk follows the route of the 'Cotswold Way' and ascends 1024 feet, 312 metres to Broadway Tower where close by rather conveniently is a large café.

The route is along farm tracks and well-defined footpaths however, depending upon the time of year some of the fields on the walk can be muddier on the descent than on the climb.

Getting There and Parking

Located on a bypass just off the A44 Evesham to Oxford Road midway between Evesham and Moreton-in-Marsh. If approaching from the south change down a gear or two as Fish Hill has quite a steep descent.

To manage the volume of tourists descending upon Broadway and to keep its picture postcard charm, on-street parking is very limited, a number of short and long stay carparks are sympathetically located around the village.

In the centre of the village tucked behind the High Street in Church Close there is a short-stay car park. Postcode WR12 7AH. A little further out along the Leamington Road is Shear House car park WR12 7ET. At the other end of the village heading out on the Cheltenham Road on the B4632 is Milestone Ground car park located on Childswickham Road. Postcode WR12 7HA. Further along Station Road is Broadway Station car park WR12 7DH. This car park is five minutes from the station and charges are £5 for ten hours parking of which £3 is redeemable towards a train ride at the station booking office.

The original railway station opened in 1904 and closed to passengers in 1960. The service today is operated by the Gloucestershire Warwickshire Steam Railway and is located on the north-western edge of the village and runs at least five trains a day (depending upon the time of year) from Cheltenham Racecourse via Toddington and Winchcombe. All day return tickets are £20 for adults. The station is approximately 3/4 mile from the centre of the village.

There is an infrequent bus service from Chipping Campden to Cheltenham on the 606 and between Stratford-upon-Avon and Moreton-in-Marsh. However, the 606 does run on a Sunday!

There are a number of other buses which run on market days only.

Maps

OS map: Explorer OL45 The Cotswolds

Broadway Map

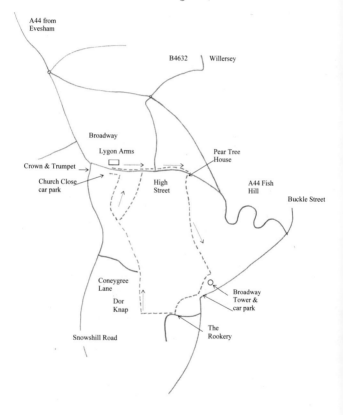

A44 from
Evesham

B4632   Willersey

Broadway

Lygon Arms

Crown & Trumpet

Church Close
car park

Pear Tree
House

High
Street

A44 Fish
Hill

Buckle Street

Coneygree
Lane

Dor
Knap

Broadway
Tower &
car park

The
Rookery

Snowshill Road

A Little Slice of History

Broadway was one of six new market towns founded in the Cotswolds after the Norman Conquest. Broadway would appear to take its name from the broad main street now renamed the High Street. The 'broad-way' was unusually wide because of two streams running down either side of the main drovers road through the village. Later the streams were enclosed in pipes thus enabling the width of the road to further increase. Up until the Reformation of 1538 Broadway was under the jurisdiction of the Benedictine Abbey of Pershore. The abbot had a substantial summer residence built for him in 1320 (now known as the Abbot's Grange) facing the Green. In the Middle Ages Broadway grew rich from the wool trade which flourished in the Cotswolds for several centuries. The prosperous merchants left their legacy of fine houses all made from the same golden coloured stone.

Nikolaus Pevsner is very complimentary of Broadway in his book 'The Buildings of England – Worcestershire', he describes it as 'the show village of England'. The High Street and Church Street with its Tudor, Stuart and Georgian architecture are happily mixed in with early twentieth-century buildings, all of which are a delight to the eye.

The impressive Lygon Arms Hotel circa 1532

was originally the White Hart Inn where during the Civil War Charles I met with his confidants and Oliver Cromwell slept at the inn, at different times of course!

In the seventeenth century Broadway became a busy coaching stop on the route between Worcester and London. With the construction of the railway network in the 1850s the coaching days came to an end and the village regained its genteel calm. With this new found peace and quiet, Broadway attracted a number of artists and writers including Elgar, John Singer Sargent, J M Barrie, Vaughan Williams, William Morris and the actress Mary Anderson.

To further soak up the local history it is worth visiting the Broadway Museum and Art Gallery which is located in the seventeenth-century Tudor House at 64-65 the High Street. It was formerly the Ashmolean Museum Broadway and explores the history and development of the town. Admission is £5 for adults and is open 10-4 in the winter and 10-5 during the summer. The website is www.broadwaymuseum.org.uk

The work of the renowned twentieth-century furniture designer, Sir Gordon Russell MC is celebrated at the Gordon Russell Museum in Russell Square in the centre of the town. Admission is £5 for adults and is open Tuesday to Sunday. The website is www.gordonrussellmuseum.org

Up on Broadway Hill is Broadway Tower, a four-storey folly inspired by Capability Brown. It was built after his death in 1798 for the Earl of Coventry and designed

by the prominent architect, James Wyatt. The tower
has accommodated a number of eclectic occupants over
the years. In 1822 Sir Thomas Phillips renowned as
the greatest collector of manuscripts in history, set
up Middle Hill Press in the tower to not only record
his book catalogue but also to publish his findings in
English topography and genealogy.

Later it was used as a country retreat by artists
William Morris, Dante Gabriel Rossetti and Edward
Burne-Jones. William Morris was so inspired by
Broadway Tower that he founded in 1877 the Society for
the Protection of Ancient Buildings. In the late 1950s it
was used to monitor nuclear fallout. An underground
Cold War bunker was built fifty yards from the Tower
and was manned between 1961 and 1991 and is still
believed to be fully equipped and maintained.

The tower is open to visitors, providing graphic
displays of its history, roof viewing platform and shop.
On a clear day It is said that thirteen counties can be
seen from the top of the tower

A short distance from the Tower at the foot of
Snowshill on an old trail down from the Cotswold
escarpment lies the twelfth century church of St
Eadburgha. An eccentric account by J Lees-Milne 'A
Shell Guide to Worcestershire' describes 'St Eadburgha,
a priggish child saint who officiously insisted on
washing other people's socks. Obviously not his most
favourite Saint! The original village of Broadway stood
here but as a new trail developed over the Cotswolds St
Eadburghas church became stranded half a mile from
the present village.

See walk 6 Pershore for further information
concerning St Eadburgha.

Refreshments

There are a limited number of pubs, and a good collection of café's and restaurants to enjoy as well as the café close to the Tower.

Where at one time thirty-three inns existed in Broadway there are as far as I can make out just three. The Crown and Trumpet in Church Street close to The Green is a splendid traditional seventeenth-century Cotswold inn serving a range of excellent ales and cider. There is the Horse and Hound at 54 the High Street and The Swan at 2 The Green. Don't go into the Lygon Arms and ask for a pint as I did, there is nothing available on tap. However, if your tipple is cocktails or wine then it's the place for you!

Along the Walk

This is very popular walk especially at weekends and Bank Holidays.

Heading Out for the Walk

On approaching the village from the south on the A44, the long stay car park on Leamington Road and the short stay car park just off the

High Street in Church Close provides easy access to the walk. Public conveniences are located in the short stay car park. The Information Board in the short stay car park provides a useful map of the area.

The walk begins in the High Street, so to get there, face towards the town, turn right out of the car park and walk past the Abbey Green vets and onto a secluded footpath for a short distance before reaching the appropriately named Kennel Lane and then turn left towards the High Street.

The impressive fourteenth-century Lygon Arms is across the broad high street which gives its name to the town. Turning to the right, spend a little time window shopping to soak up the charming atmosphere of this affluent High Street.

Continue away from the town ignoring the footpath by the impressive 17th century Tudor House which contains the Broadway Museum and Art Gallery. On reaching the roundabout carry straight on as indicated by the signpost pointing to the 'Cotswold Way' up this tranquil section of the High Street.

Continue past the United Reformed Church and walk up the High Street to number 111, Pear Tree House where the wooden Broadway Tower/Cotswold Way footpath sign points to the right.

Pear Tree House was built before 1772 by Sir Edward Winnington Lord of the Manor of Broadway. Follow the little driveway to a wooden swing gate where there is a sign informing you to keep your dog on a lead.

Head into the field through a galvanised swing gate following the well-trodden path over a brook where upon there is a steady uphill climb. Plenty of wooden posts indicate the route to follow.

Continue uphill through a swing gate with a tiny sign 'Broadway Trust'. Head up across the next

field where sheep may be grazing to the next wooden swing gate. Following the stone wall to your left continue uphill to a viewing point where three optimally placed wooden seats have been located.

Keeping close to the stone wall which later on peters out to wire fencing, the impressive Broadway Tower can be seen on the skyline. After the final climb of the day, go through the large wrought iron gate into the Broadway Tower Country Park.

Here next to the Tower there are magnificent views for a radius of sixty-two miles across Worcestershire and a further fifteen counties. Admission tickets for the Tower can be purchased from the cafe a little further on.

A little distance past the tower on the escarpment there is a plaque to the five-airman

killed in 1943 when their RAF bomber crashed here.

Continue along the path towards the pay and display car park, Morris & Brown café and ticket office for the Tower.

The public footpath continues to the right of the café

next to a red deer compound. If not stopping for a break continue through a metal gate and small field onto a narrow lane. The 'Private no entry' sign applies to vehicles only as you continue down towards the rather imposing Cotswold farmhouse on the right.

The lane continues round to the left but the footpath heads downhill with Rookery Farm to the right. Continue past the entrance to the Shepherds Huts to a T junction of tracks. Take the right track traversing the hillside with the impressive but unusually named building Dor Knap down below.

Note the attractive Fox shaped weathervane on the last cottage down the track. The path continues to traverse the hillside towards a small copse, go through two metal gates at the top of Coneygree Lane. Ignore the main track heading slightly uphill towards the woods but head left downhill at 45° following the small path to the far bottom left hand corner of the field. Continue across the next field on the same tack to a rickety stile next to a wooden seat which was erected some years before the Millennium Woods were planted by the Cotswold voluntary wardens thus blocking any view to be had.

The path can be a little ill-defined but keep heading in the direction of the church steeple in Broadway. Cross over the stile and a little further down by a small farm building the footpath to Broadway Museum and Art Gallery is crossed. Either return via this route or continue down the field with the hedgerow to the left, to a stream and stone bridge where there is chance to clean off muddy boots.

There are a number of footpaths at this point, either head back onto the High Street or continue past a couple of small industrial units and then past the Collins Family butchers which sells quite delicious pies before entering the short footpath which then leads to the Abbey Green vets and car park.

Waypoints

Church Close short-stay car park SP 09564 37358

High Street opposite the Lygon Arms SP 09675 37524

111 the High Street start of footpath SP 10187 37598

Wooden seats with view next to the footpath SP 10765 36729

Broadway Tower SP 11369 36212

T junction of tracks SP 10749 35702

Coneygree Lane SP 10698 36143

Millennium Woods SP 10304 36713

Small farm building SP 10055 37100

Stream and stone bridge SP 09685 37187

Notes and Observations from This Walk

Walk Two
Elmley Castle to Bredon Hill

Summary

The quiet picturesque village of Elmley Castle nestles beneath the northern slopes of Bredon Hill and is the starting point for this fairly strenuous 4.8 mile/7.7 km distance walk. Bredon Hill is the largest of the Cotswold 'outliers' and commands an impressive view across the Severn Valley. The walk joins the Wychavon Way for a short distance. This long-distance footpath was originally opened in 1977 to commemorate the Silver Jubilee of Queen Elizabeth II. In 2012 the route was revised to start at Droitwich Spa and now finishes at Broadway. The waymarkers depict a green hill above a horizontally stretched V-shaped blue river. The walk culminates in reaching the Banbury Stone tower providing an opportunity to experience the magnificent views across the River Avon and Severn Valley and south-west towards the Forest of Dean and the Vale of Gloucester.

Getting There and Parking

The village can be approached from Pershore, Evesham and Ashton-under-Hill. From junction 7 of the M5 head towards Pershore on the A44. Continue through Pershore in the Evesham direction and turn right just after the bridge over the River Avon and then immediately fork left where it is signposted Elmley

Castle. From the south, junction 8 it is a little more convoluted, take the M50 to junction 1 Malvern turn off. On the exit road as the roundabout is approached there is a turning left to the pleasant village of Twyning. On approaching the village green there is a left turning for Strensham. Follow this twisting and turning minor road towards Defford and then turn right for Pershore.

With respect to parking, there is limited space on Main Street near the Queen Elizabeth public house especially over the weekend. However, there is the delightfully located Worcestershire County Council car park and picnic place just off the Main Street in the Ashton-under-Hill direction in Kersoe Lane. Postcode WR10 3HS and map reference SO 98434 41023.

The only public transport service is the 564 bus between Evesham and Pershore. It stops three times a day on Saturdays and four times per day during the week to accommodate the local schools. There is no Sunday service.

Maps

Bredon Hill Map

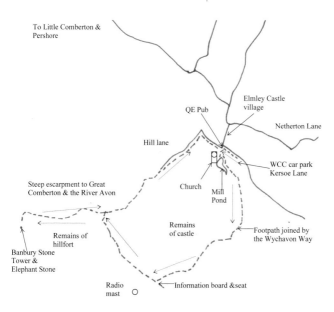

To Little Comberton & Pershore

Elmley Castle village

QE Pub

Netherton Lane

Hill lane

WCC car park
Kersoe Lane

Steep escarpment to Great Comberton & the River Avon

Church

Mill Pond

Remains of castle

Footpath joined by the Wychavon Way

Remains of hillfort

Banbury Stone
Tower &
Elephant Stone

Radio mast

Information board & seat

A Little Slice of History

The village derives its name from the castle that was built on the hillside during the Norman occupation in 1080. The castle was once home to the D'Abitots and Beauchamps whose names are also closely linked to the Worcestershire village of Redmarley D'Abitot. By the early 1400s it was in ruins. The remains of the castle are on private fenced off grounds, but it is said there are just foundations remaining as most of the stone was used to construct Pershore Bridge, local churches and the alike.

The Norman church of St Mary has a fortified tower and battlements. Inside there is a thirteenth-century carved stone font and three attractive alabaster effigies of the Savage family who became Lords of the Manor during the reign of Henry VIII.

The figures are in good condition with gilded detail on their costumes. The second large monument in the church is for the Earl of Coventry (for more details see the Croome walk in book 3) who died in 1699.

In the churchyard there are two unusual sundials

dating from the sixteenth century, one which depicts the Savage family coat of arms.

Bredon Hill has been the inspiration to a multitude of poets, writers, artists and composers due to its eclectic mix of history going back to pagan times, the folklore surrounding the standing stones and the awe-inspiring views.

The hill is immortalised in A E Houseman's 1896 anthology 'A Shropshire Lad'. Which begins:

> In summertime on Bredon
> The bells they sound so clear;
> Round both the shires they ring them
> In steeples far and near,
> A happy noise to hear.

The Folly on Bredon Hill is described on the OS map as the Banbury Stone Tower and is the most visible landmark for a great many miles. The Tower is also called Parsons Folly and it is believed to have been built in the mid-eighteenth century for John Parsons who was the squire of Kemerton Court. The tower is thirty-nine feet high and takes the combined hill and tower to an overall height of 1,000 feet/305 m. The tower is now used as a mobile phone base station.

Just below the Tower is the Banbury Stone which is also known because of its shape as the Elephant Stone. This unusual shaped standing stone and the nearby King and Queen Stones have healing folklore attached to them. It is the tradition on Good Friday to kiss the Banbury Stone for good luck. A Christian service is also held here on Good Friday.

The Tower is located on one of the three Iron Age Hillforts on Bredon Hill known as Kemerton Camp. There are two sets of ramparts and ditches to the south of the Tower. In the 1930s excavations revealed the remains of fifty slaughtered men and a great number of weapons.

Refreshments

In the 1980s there were three pubs in Elmly, now the only survivor is the rather fine and popular Queen Elizabeth public house, and is so named following a stay by Queen Elizabeth I

Along the Walk

There are very likely to be sheep in some fields nearby and two stiles to navigate

Heading Out for the Walk

If you have parked at the Worcestershire County Council car park opposite the cricket pitch and children's play area walk back towards the village.

Turn to the left towards St Marys and Elmley Castle church. On the opposite side of the road is

the Queen Elizabeth public house, the only hostelry on this walk and well worth a visit. The waymarker next to the old wooden churchyard gates points across the churchyard and past the church. Do take time to admire the two mid-sixteenth century sundials.

The footpath goes left of the church and through a small copse and alongside a mill pond. Coming out of the copse the path passes through paddocks and after a short distance meets a large ploughed field.

The OS map indicates a footpath across the middle of the field. However, it is better not to annoy the farmer and stick to the right-hand field boundary. There is a stile about two-thirds the way along the field next to a tree stump. It's very

easy to miss in the height of summer. Once over the stile the path heads left at 45° to the next field boundary. If this stile is missed, no worries, as at the far side of the field there is another stile following a small bridge made out of planks of wood across the ditch. Simply turn right heading up hill to meet the first path. There is a bridleway sign indicating the Wychavon Way at this junction of paths. The route is as you would expect uphill and unfortunately can be a little muddy in places.

As height is gained there are options to take a number of slightly different tracks. Passing an old stone wall the path continues uphill alongside a sturdy fence. This is to keep folk away from visiting the ruins of Elmley Castle. The brief glimpses of the castle

through the trees indicates
there are only footings and
foundations remaining in
any case. The broad track
continues up through the
woods and onto the plateau
where an information
board and wooden seat have been
located to enhance the experience
of the views towards the Cotswolds.
To the far left is a steel tower
festooned with aerials.

Turning to the right alongside the woods follow
the well-worn path to a gate. At this juncture the path
downhill to the right is for the return journey. Continue
straight on as the scenery opens out with expansive
views off to the right towards Elmley Castle. As the
path circumnavigates Bredon Hill Pershore is in the

distance and the River
Avon twists and turns
around Birlingham and
Great Comberton as it flows
towards the River Severn at
Tewkesbury.

The path runs alongside the stone wall where on the other side the hillside descends quite steeply towards Great Comberton. A short distance further on to the left is a small copse and a gate. In the distance the Banbury Stone Tower can be seen. To the left covering a considerable area are the substantial earth works of the ancient hillfort. Just below and to the right of the tower is the much-photographed large elephant shaped rock. The views across the plain to the Malvern Hills are quite spectacular.

The return journey retraces the route alongside the stone wall and escarpment to the woods encompassing the remains of Elmley Castle where the broad path provides an easy descent. Continue downhill and through the gate and across the heathland to a galvanised swing gate which leads into a culvert lined with trees. After a short distance the path meets the top end of the single-track, Hill Lane. Continue towards the village for approximately 0.6 of a mile where the welcoming beer garden of the Queen Elizabeth public house is reached. Possibly a good time to avail yourself of a welcome refreshment at the end of this invigorating walk on Bredon Hill.

Waypoints

Elmley Castle, Worcestershire County Council, Kersoe Lane car park and picnic area: SO 98434 41023

Entrance to large ploughed field: SO 98318 40905

Far side of the ploughed field crossing a small ditch: SO 98548 40569

Bridleway sign: SO 98479 40255

Old stone wall: SO 97993 39887

Wooden seat and information board: SO 97369 39542

Small copse: SO 96271 40303

Banbury Tower: SO 95676 40212 939 ft

Path down for the return journey: five-barred metal gate: SO 96716 40253 895ft

Gate midway to Hill Lane: SO 97087 40520

Top of Hill Lane: SO 97434 40856 -406ft

Notes and Observations from This Walk

Walk Three
Upton upon Severn

Summary

A 4.3 mile/6.9 km circular walk. Allow approximately two hours without stops. In general, it is easy walking with no hills to speak of. My GPS device recorded a height gain of just thirty metres! It can be muddy in places and has a few stiles to navigate. There is a strong likelihood of cattle and or sheep grazing on the Ham, so dog walkers exercise caution. Upton has a significant number of hostelries and café's which not only keep the locals very happy but accommodate for the frequent influx of festival goers and those enjoying this walk.

Upton upon Severn is a small vibrant town which according to the 2011 census recorded a population of just 2,881 making it the smallest town in the county. It is located on the western bank of the River Severn. Adjacent is Fish Meadow which provides a large riverside venue for events such as the Jazz and Blues Festivals and in recent years the Sunshine popular music festival which has grown considerably in size.

According to the BBC News, Upton upon Severn has been dubbed 'the most flooded town in Britain'. Upton has seen flooding seventy-eight times since 1970, according to the Environment Agency. There are flood height markers recording the highest flood levels on the boundary wall to the Pepperpot in the High Street and on the wall of the parish church of St Peter and St Paul in Old Street. Following a couple of years of road restrictions and long queues, flood defences were built near to Fish Meadow. However, the area opposite the Regal Garage and car park which has not undergone any flood defences could well cause Upton to be closed as happened in 2007, 2012 and 2020.

Getting There and Parking

Upton is situated mid-way between Worcester and Tewkesbury. From the south the M50 junction 1 provides access via the A38 Worcester road and then turn left onto the A4104. The B4211 Gloucester to Worcester road is the main thoroughfare through Upton and provides a delightfully scenic route into Upton. If approaching from the southern end of the Malvern's or Ledbury the A4104 via Welland is straightforward. To the west of the River Severn the B4211 is accessed from the Worcester ring road at

Powick. If visiting the Three Counties Showground, Upton is a shade over five miles.

Prior to 1961 you could take the train to Upton. The nearest railway station is now Great Malvern some 6.5 miles away. A number of buses infrequently connect with Upton. The 332 has just one return journey to Worcester per day, the 333 is again just one return journey, the 363 has six services a day to Worcester, the 365 has one return service to Malvern and the 481 has one service connecting to Ledbury and Cheltenham per day.

Upton provides the only opportunity to cross the River Severn for the sixteen-mile stretch between Worcester and Tewkesbury (with the exception of the M50) and therefore can be very busy when events in Upton or at the Three Counties Showground near Malvern are taking place.

Probably the best place to park if undertaking this walk is the free car park next to the rugby club in Old Street just along the narrow High Street heading in the direction of Gloucester. Access to the Old Street car park (note the height restriction) is opposite the church of St Peter and St Paul at SO 85073, 40300. WR8 0HW. On street parking in Upton is limited to an hour.

Alternatively, there is a large pay and display car park including public toilets near the centre of the town a hundred or so metres past the impressive Regal Garage on the

B4211 Hanley Road close to the river bridge At SO 85010, 40786. WR8 0HY.

Maps

OS map: Explorer 190 Malvern Hills & Bredon Hill.

Upton Map

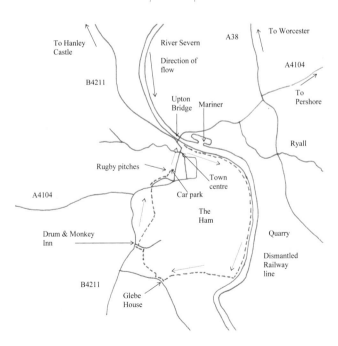

A Little Slice of History

On the corner of School Lane and Brown Square lies a block of basalt embedded into the roadside. It is believed to originate from North Wales and arrived here during prehistoric times courtesy of an iceberg!

When the Romans invaded Britain, it would appear they were not too concerned with the villages of Upton, Hanley or Malvern, however in 1787 a shepherd boy found a circular cavity in a cornfield which led to an underground cavern of considerable dimensions. It is said that the water in it went to a depth of 140 feet. A number of similar caverns have been found in Germany following the Roman occupation which led to the theory it was Roman built. Unfortunately, there is no indication where this cavern was located but it would be very interesting to find it!

Although the Danes invaded Tewkesbury just a few miles downstream it is not known whether Upton suffered the same fate. The Domesday Book indicates that in 1086 the average income from the manor had remained the same for twenty years. Maintaining its value whilst neighbouring Hanley Castle declined in value. This would indicate that the river trade was of incalculable commercial importance in Upton's continued development, providing employment in salmon fishing and associated trades.

The Bishop of Hereford in 1289 had his wine sent from the port of Bristol up the Severn to Upton then

carried by land to his palace. The wharf in Upton
handled the export of pottery and utensils from Hanley
Castle which was the local centre of the medieval pottery
industry. The boats used to convey the goods were
flat-bottomed sailing ships called trows which could
carry up to 120 tons and small trows carried forty
tons. Up to 1812 the trows had been pulled by men when
sailing was difficult however with the construction of a
horse drawn towing path between Worcester and Lower
Parting (close to Gloucester) there was a revolt by the
locals as livelihoods were threatened by the introduction
of this faster more efficient method of moving goods
along the river.

By the nineteenth century the Severn was busy
carrying great quantities of cider, corn and coal.
In particular a great deal of Herefordshire cider was
transported from Upton. The Severn is not tidal at
Upton, the nearest point being Gloucester. By the later
nineteenth century steam tugs had taken over much
of the river transport. Transportation on the river came
under threat when in 1864 Upton railway station
opened on the Malvern to Tewkesbury line signifying
the days of river transport were numbered.

Given that Upton is ten miles downstream from
Worcester and eighteen miles upstream from Gloucester
it is not surprising that the development of the bridge
across the River Severn was so strategically important.
The first bridge in Upton was built towards the end
of the fifteenth century, by 1606 a substantial red
sandstone bridge had replaced the earlier wooden bridge.
In 1646 the arch nearest the town was destroyed in
an attempt to block the advancing Parliamentarians.
Planks were laid across the gap to enable the townsfolk

to go about their business but carelessly were still in place when Oliver Cromwell's soldiers arrived. The Royalists attacked but were defeated at the Battle of Upton enabling Cromwell to march onto Worcester for the final battle of the English Civil War.

The bridge must have been quite substantial because it was documented in 1733 that John Dickins had a pig sty on it! By the end of the nineteenth century the bridge was in a poor state of repair and in 1833 the bridge was replaced by a swing bridge. The abutments can still be seen today by the Kings Head and on the opposite bank of the river.

The current steel bridge was constructed in 1939. But more recently in 2011 controversy raged as following a six-week public consultation by the county council as to what colour the bridge should be painted. The chosen colour scheme by the public was duchess blue with gold trim, but rather oddly it ended up being painted bright yellow! It indeed looked awful. The bridge was finally repainted in the correct colours but not without weeks of frustration at the bridge's closure due to the two attempts at painting it!

John Dee (1527–1608) was appointed rector of the parish church of St Peter and St Paul. His early career as a mathematician won him deserved fame and respect for his work on Euclid. Elizabeth I had great faith in him as an astrologer. However, it is not clear whether he ever came to Upton! By 1580 he had become obsessed with spiritualism and aroused suspicion and resentment. He died in poverty at Mortlake.

The original parish church of St Peter and St Paul has had a chequered history. Even before the English Civil War the church tower which is thought to date from the fourteenth century and its base from the thirteenth century was apparently in a poor state of repair. In 1651 the church was considerably damaged during the Battle of Upton. During 1754 the nave was rebuilt. However, by 1770 the spire was considered unsafe and following this it was pulled down by a body of men who were roped to the spire across the river. A copper cupola replaced the spire giving it the peculiar pepper pot shape. In the 1820s more galleries were added but concern was expressed over the structural safety of the building. The church remained in a poor condition and was rather too small for the size of the congregation. Therefore, a larger plot was needed and in 1879 the current church of St Peter and St Paul was consecrated and located in Old Street. One of the icons salvaged from the old church is the crusader knights tomb which probably originated in the late thirteenth or early fourteenth century. It is

believed to be a member of the Boteler family who held land in Upton. During the move his legs were lost, he now resides beneath a Roll of Honour to the rear of the church.

Moving back into the centre of the town of historical note is the prominent White Lion Inn where a number of chapters of Henry Fielding's 'Tom Jones' is set. The book was published in 1749 and is among the earliest English prose works to be classified as a novel.

A little further towards the river is Dunns Lane where after a few yards a blue plaque above a tiny alleyway depicts the first victim of a cholera outbreak in 1832. The cholera burial ground is a little way out of town on the minor road towards The Hook.

One cannot fail to notice the impressive looking Regal Garage. The garage was once the cider and vinegar works of the Kent family

from 1778. Imported foreign wine and spirits were also sold here after being unloaded from the wharf just across the road.

John Wesley visited the town twice to preach between 1768 and 1770. Along School Lane is St Joseph's Roman Catholic church designed by Charles Hansom, who was the brother of Joseph the designer of the Hansom cab.

In the grounds of the Pepperpot is the elegant bust of Sir William Tennant (1890-1963) who was born in Upton. He served in the Royal Navy in both World Wars and was the British Commander during the evacuation of Dunkirk.

Refreshments

Upton has an unusually high ratio of watering holes and cafés per head of population to experience. The Drum and Monkey at Newbridge Green is also located close to this scenic walk.

Along the Walk

From the 1st of August until the following January sheep will most likely be grazing on the Hams and it is advised that between March and July care be taken to protect

ground-nesting birds such as skylarks. There are also a couple of stiles to navigate.

Heading Out for the Walk

The walk starts from either of the two car parks in Upton and meanders through the town before following the river along the Severn Way footpath. Bridleways and footpaths complete the rest of the relatively flat return journey, although it can be a little muddy in places.

If starting from the Hanley Road car park walk past the impressive Art Deco styled Regal Garage and over the roundabout, then follow the text from the paragraph beginning with 'Straight on is the High Street'.

The information board at the entrance to the Old Street free car park provides a good overview of the local landmarks. Cross over the road and on the left-hand stone gate pillar on the wall of the parish church of St Peter and St Paul the flood level for March 1947 is indicated.

This church was

built in 1879 to replace
the original, the iconic
Pepperpot in the centre of
town which was deemed to
be unsafe and too small
for its parishioners. Take
the time to visit the church
where at the back of the
church is the effigy of
a fourteenth-century
crusader knight grasping
a sword. He was a local
man William Boteler.
He and his brother were
involved in building
the fourteenth century
church. During the move
from the Pepperpot his
legs somehow became
detached from his body
and were lost. I promise
no puns about legless

Will! Above him is the Red Cross flag of the Voluntary
Aid Detachment (VAD) which was a voluntary unit of
civilians providing nursing care for military personnel
from the First World War.

Walk towards the town passing the Muggery public
house on the left which has an interesting range of
vegetarian and traditional meals such as Diddy Dan
pie and a ceiling festooned with mugs.

It is good to see a number of traditional shops still
in business and over the years the antique trade in
Upton has become quite established.

Cross over New Street and over to the right is the White Lion Hotel which was the setting for Henry Fielding's, 'A History of Tom Jones'.

Along the parade of shops is the Upton Map Shop. This is well known and provides a comprehensive cartography service as well as stocking a wide range of travel books (including this one).

Straight on, the High Street heads towards the river, turn left at this junction into Church Street and approximately eighty metres towards the roundabout and road bridge there is a small blue plaque on the side of a Georgian House depicting where on 29 August 1651 Oliver Cromwell was greeted here by an 'abundance of joy and extraordinary shouting', after the decisive battle of Upton.

Just a few paces further on is the fascinating Tudor House museum. Opposite is the oldest surviving building in Upton, the unusual Pepperpot and

adjoining it the Tourist Information and Heritage Centre. In 1651 the church was considerably damaged when the Parliamentary forces crossed the river and attacked the Royalists during the Battle of Upton. The defeat of the Royalist and the loss of this important river crossing put Charles II at a strategic disadvantage leading to his defeat shortly afterwards at the Battle of Worcester.

After visiting the Pepperpot, head in the direction of the bridge

where there is a delightful row of pretty cottages which lead down towards the Plough Inn and river. With the road bridge to the left there is a short flight of steps heading down to the river through the flood defences. Look underneath the bridge where there is an attractive blue painted seat themed on the 'Upton Blues Festival'.

Continue past The Kings Head with its attractive beer terrace overlooking the river. To the right is the High Street, public conveniences and just a little further on the stone-faced boundary wall of the Pepperpot, where there are little diamond plaques depicting flood levels in 1852 and 1886.

Returning to the river over on the opposite bank the entrance to Upton Marina and to the right a small jetty where the leisure cruiser, MV Conway Castle provides scenic Sunday lunch, fish and chip, evening cruises and a waterbus service along the river to Worcester and Tewksbury.

Opposite the jetty above the Severn Leisure Cruises offices is the Boathouse Tapas Bar with a wonderful view of the river. Continuing along the river and past the third hostelry on this short stretch of river, the popular Swan Hotel and its delightful al fresco seating. The impressive Georgian 'Waterside House' with its attractive walled garden is adjacent to the front entrance to the hotel. The riverside walk continues along the tree lined Dunn's Lane through an iron gate to the Severn Way footpath where a superb view opens out across a substantial area of flood plain known as Upper Ham. The word Ham is derived from the Old English word 'hamm' meaning a meadow.

An information board describes these fields as Lammas Fields meaning that commoners share the right to graze cattle here from the 1st of August until the following January. The Lammas system has been in place for over a thousand years. With such a large flat area it is not unsurprising that in 1883 there was a thousand-yard rifle range here.

The Severn Way public footpath follows the riverbank. After walking for fifteen minutes or so from the town centre on the opposite bank there is a water treatment plant and a little further on barges are loaded up with sand from a quarry. The view across to the Malvern's and back to Upton is quite outstanding.

At the end of this extensive field there is a five-barred wooden gate where there is an information board describing 'Upton Ham site of special scenic interest'.

On reaching the next field boundary there are the remains of the old embankment for the Malvern to Tewkesbury railway bridge. Evidence of brick supports for the bridge can be seen on the opposite side of the bank. The line closed to passenger traffic in 1961. The span across the river here is 145 yards. The bridge had five sections and incorporated a sliding section to allow tall-masted sailing ships to pass through. A chain driven mechanism to move the sliding section was located on the riverbank and fell out of use during the 1930s.

Continue following the Severn Way and where the river begins to bend to the right a stile is reached. Once over the stile keeping the field boundary hedgerow to the right, head away from the river to a metal gate and farm buildings in the distance. Do note there is no footpath waymarker indicating the route. Referring to the OS Explorer map 190 the route is indicated above the wording 'Lower Ham'.

Head towards a small rise in the land towards a seven-bar metal gate which leads onto a muddy farm track. Follow the farm track with a copse to the right past a couple of fields where there are some very fine-looking horses.

The farm track reaches a lane where to the left is Glebe House. Turn right and then just a few metres further on there is a footpath sign on the right-hand side which points along a driveway and towards open fields where there are several footpath signs. One indicates left along the field boundary next to garden and one signpost points straight on. Our route to the Drum and Monkey at Newbridge Green is half left (northwest) past a large oak tree and towards a five-barred metal gate into the next field.

On reaching the gate keep this side of it and follow the hedgerow to the right towards a lane and a copse to the right. The footpath comes out onto the lane over a stile by a house called Steeple View. The Drum and Monkey public house is over to the left on the B4211 at Newbridge Green.

Following a visit to this local hostelry return back down the lane a short distance to 'The Cottage' on the left-hand corner of the lane. Then follow the track past farm buildings to the left onto a gate where there is a ditch to the right. Continue over the stile along the grassy path, a row of trees separates the farm buildings from the path. Ahead in the distance a church steeple comes into view. Continue along the right-hand side of the field. On reaching the corner of the field go straight on over a stile and then follow the path down the bank onto a substantial track.

There are large fields to the right with Bredon Hill in the distance. The Pepperpot can be seen ahead as the noise of cars on the main road becomes discernible. The well-used broad track leads to a metal swing gate next to the main road. The modern Upton Medical Centre is opposite. Turn to the right and cross over the road and follow the pavement a short distance to an old rowing boat filled with flowers.

Turn to the left along the old road which further on is used as a coach park. Ignore the footpath which appears to be in the middle of the hedge and continue to a clearly defined black kissing gate with a barrier to stop large vehicles driving into the fields ahead. The hedge is to the left with rugby pitches to the right.

There is a ditch to the left and the disused embankment of the old railway line. A little further the rugby club can be seen to the right with the Hanley Road car park completing this scenic walk around Upton.

Waypoints

Hanley Road car park: SO 85011 40787

Old Street car park: SO 85011 40787

Junction of Church Street and the High Street: SO 85190 40658

Outside the Plough Inn: SO 85155 40741

Dunn's Lane by the gate into the fields: SO 85543 40590

Old railway line crossing by the river: SO86269 39061

Stile by bend in the river: SO 86097 38649

Glebe House: SO 84853 38629

Drum and Monkey Pub: SO 84463 39179

Gate by ditch after farm: SO 84771 39599

Opposite Upton Medical Centre: SO 84705 40066

Entrance to rugby fields: SO 84895 40199

Notes and Observations from This Walk

Walk Four
Eckington Bridge

Summary

Included here are two delightful walks which can be joined together to provide a reasonably long walk of ten miles/16 km around the flood plain of the River Avon and onto the lower slopes of Bredon Hill. The walks encompass the quiet rural villages of Great Comberton, Birlingham and Eckington.

Getting There and Parking

The two circular walks enable the start and finish location to be at a point of your choosing. Eckington being the largest of the three villages does at least provide a couple of watering holes and convenience stores which might sway your choice. However, located next to the bridge at Eckington (map reference SO 92221 42257), there is a free car park and picnic area which is where the text for these walks commence. Pershore is four miles north of Eckington and Tewkesbury eight miles to the south. Access from the A4104 Upton to Pershore road is a little way outside the village of Defford.

With respect to local transport the number 54 bus to and from Worcester provides the school run, the 565 Pershore, Elmley Castle, Evesham and Pershore provides two buses per day Monday to Saturday and the 575 Pershore to Cheltenham is one return journey on Fridays only.

OS map: Explorer 190 Malvern Hills & Bredon Hill.

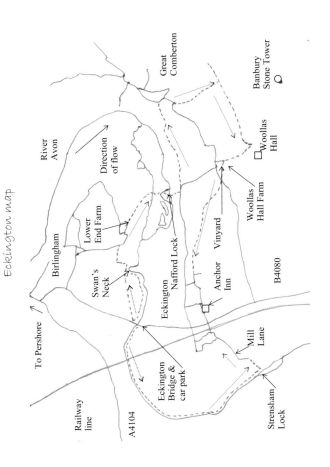

Eckington map

A Little Slice of History

The present Eckington Bridge was built in 1728. It is constructed from sandstone and has been designated as a Grade 2 listed ancient monument. The village of Great Comberton dates back to Saxon times and is mentioned in the Domesday Book.

Refreshments

On my visits to Birlingham I missed the Swan Inn which is at the other end of the village located in Church Street. Postcode WR10 3AQ. It appears to have great reviews and is well known for its range of fish dishes. Great Comberton appears to be bereft of any commercialisation which I am sure adds to its charm. Eckington being the largest of three villages does have the Bell and Anchor Inns and the Eckington Village Store, and that, folks, is about it.

Along the Walk

The two walks look like the number eight laying on its side with its centre being Eckington Bridge.

The bridge and adjoining picnic area and car park is approximately half a mile north of Eckington. The western or 5.6 km left-hand section of our figure of eight is mostly along a large loop of the river providing flat easy walking. The other loop is 10.4 km long and easy going to the lock at Nafford although the track towards the lock can be very muddy. The section of the walk into Great Comberton is across undulating ground and where there is likely to be sheep about. The route out of Great Comberton and back to Eckington climbs up the lower slope of Bredon Hill providing extensive views across the Avon floodplain. This is the only walk in the twenty-four walks featured in the two Worcestershire books that crosses a river via a lock gate. Although if you wished there are thirty locks to crisscross the Worcester & Birmingham canal in the Tardibigge walk in volume two!

Heading Out for the Walk

The delightful tiny sandstone bride at Eckington with the adjacent car park, picnic spot and wharf for public moorings is an ideal start and finish point for this walk.

73

The footpath for the first leg of this walk is across the road and down alongside the Avon riverbank. As mentioned previously the flow of the Avon just dawdles along whereas the Severn is a river on a mission. The footpath follows the barely perceptible downstream flow of the river. Ahead the train bridge for the Bristol to Birmingham line dominates the view across the flood plain. Continue under the train bridge.

Unlike my memories as a child walking under a train bridge at the same time a train thunders past overhead and being terrified out of my wits (if memory serves me, the bridge in question was under the main line from Euston to Birmingham and I was on my way to catch minnows in the Grand Union Canal next to the original Ovaltine factory). This is nothing like that as the train line is quite some vertical distance away.

Returning from my childhood memories, the path follows this large sweep of the river. The picture shows some unusual masonry on the ground by the stile, but I cannot believe this is original. If it's still there on your walk let me know your thoughts.

The countryside is delightful with plenty of distant views. Strensham lock is soon reached where the access road to the left provides the route towards the village of Eckington via Mill Lane. Even the walk into the village has a quiet almost sleepy feel about it. The route is to go over the railway bridge where it looks like Beeching cut this village off from civilisation in 1965. On meeting the main Pershore to Tewkesbury Road, turn left towards the village shop and Bell Inn.

Continue along the road where on the right

is the Holy Trinity church and further on a traditional red phone box which has been converted to a free lending library. To the right there is Eckington cemetery.

The route follows the roadside path where for the final hundred or so metres down to the bridge the path is separated from the road by a sizeable hedgerow. Once back at the bridge there is either an opportunity for a break or undertake part two of the walk.

The next section of the walk heads over the tiny stone bridge, fortunately there are pedestrian passing places built above the rising cut waters which allow for some modicum of safety when cars are also driving over the bridge.

The footpath route is across the field towards the 'Swan's Neck' in the river as marked on the OS map. However, there is also a path alongside the riverbank. On approaching the field boundary go through the five-barred gate and turn to the right where the footpath leads via a dogleg towards the southern end of the village of Birlingham leaving the river a way off to the right.

On reaching the minor road named Broadway on the map turn right heading downhill and

follow the road where it sweeps round to the left. There is soon to the left a short footpath which cuts off this bend and provides an interesting view of the gardens of quite some delightful cottages. The footpath returns to the road where the path now turns off to the right leaving the minor road along a farm track. On one occasion the track was dry but on two other visits there was a lot of deep puddles and mud. The track leads down towards the Nafford lock gates and weir providing a little oasis of water courses, weirs and lock gates. Cross over the tiny canal like bridge towards the substantial weir.

Leaving the sound of rushing water behind head

straight up the incline of the ridge of the flood plain where the minor Nafford Road is met. To turn right leads back into Eckington. Turning left along the road for a short distance where, as the road turns a sharp right the footpath continues straight on across the fields.

Over to the left the expanse of the flood plain is apparent. On one visit during a very hot Easter there were cattle with black hides looking somewhat like water buffalo enjoying a bathe in the pools of water in the low-lying flood plain. If you knew no better, you would swear you had been transported to Africa in the middle of the Serengeti.

The footpath follows the contours of the fields and just drops below the next field boundary where it can be seen from the fleece left behind in the Hawthorns, sheep have been present. The path heads slightly downhill towards a gate where the path exits the fields up a steep gradient towards the tiny village of Great Comberton. The footpath joins a minor road where opposite across a field the

local churchyard of St Michael and All Angels dominates. Turn to the right along this quiet C road where shortly it dips downhill where a footpath sign peeks through the trees.

This is the afore mentioned uphill section of the walk. The path follows a field boundary to the left and more or less is straight up towards a woodland section on Bredon Hill passing over a stile and through a swing gate. On meeting a track circumnavigating this side of the hill, turn in the homeward direction to the right and follow the track. There are fine views across the Avon valley.

Crossing several field boundaries the track heads towards a splendid-looking house marked Woollas Hall on the OS map, where shortly before the hall the footpath waymarker points downhill across the

pasture to the service lane to the farm. Join the lane heading downhill passing Woollas Hall Farm on the left. On passing Wollass Hall Farm buildings a driveway signposted Wollass Hall turns to the left.

A Waymarker also indicates the route. Continue along the driveway a short distance where off to the right a gate leads down across a field towards the Deerpark Wine Vineyard.

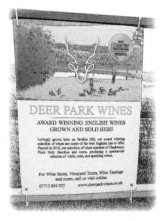

The vineyard sales outlet is along the drive to the left through a small car park. The path leads down to the next gate which looks like it might have been fashioned from an an old set of turnstiles rescued from an ailing football club.

The path clearly passes down through the well-manicured vines to the stile in the field boundary with the lane.

I must confess I was quite excited when I saw the vineyard as this is the first vineyard to appear in my Pictorial Guides. Cross over the lane to the opposite stile where the Waymarker points across the field. However, most of the footprints left by previous walkers bear left more or less following the field boundary which on the lower section can be muddy. A couple of planks bridge the ditch to a shiny galvanised gate.

The path heads up

and across a substantial
field towards the field
boundary. Off to the far
right are farm buildings
on the Nafford Road.
As the hedgerow is met
the next galvanised gate
is directly ahead. Cross
this small field where
the path runs parallel to
the hedgerow and to the
final galvanised gate
of the walk. Continue a
short distance along this
secluded path where Upper
End farm buildings can
be glimpsed to the left. A
Waymarker points back
in the direction we have
just walked and another
Waymarker points
across a field towards the
Nafford Road.

On meeting Upper End
Lane continue straight
on. Bredon Hill is off
to the left. Upper End now joins Hacketts Lane keep
straight on with Stony Furlong Lane off to the left
a little further on. The lane sweeps round to the right
changings its name to Pass Street. Turn left into
School Lane. The Primary school is on the left and the
village hall to the right. Towards the end of the lane
are some rather fine houses. Take the left-hand dog leg

down to Cotheridge Lane with Jarvis Street off to the right.

One might best advised to avoid the school day start or finish times during term time as it becomes very busy with parents and their offspring. The rather fine Anchor Inn is a little further down on the right.

A very short distance further on is the B4080 Tewkesbury Road. Turn right past the village stores with Station Gardens opposite. Here there is a choice. Either continue through Eckington back to the bridge car park or undertake the shorter loop back to the bridge via Station Gardens and the River Avon as described (in reverse) at the beginning of this walk.

Waypoints

First walk
Eckington Bridge car park and picnic area: SO 92221 42257
Railway Bridge: SO 91745 42453
Strensham Lock: SO 91519 40483
Railway Bridge in Eckington: SO 92173 41224

Second walk
Swan Neck: SO 92957 42430
Minor road indicated as Broadway on OS map: SO 93331 42579
Farm track towards Nafford lock: SO 93649 42464

Nafford lock and weir: SO 94085 41944
Footpath off the Nafford Road: SO 94182 41693
Great Comberton: SO 95364 42040
Bredon Hill meeting a transverse track: SO 95699 41109
Near Woollas Hall: SO 94894 40759
Footpath through Woollas Hall Farm: SO 94528 41019
Entrance to large ploughed field: SO 93862 41328
Upper End Farm: SO 93088 41474

Notes and Observations from This Walk

Walk Five
The Hanleys

Summary

A delightful 5 mile/8 km walk through some of Worcestershire's finest countryside with superb views towards the Malvern Hills. Hanley Castle is now a tiny hamlet but was once strategically important as the administrative centre for the Malvern Chase area. The castle component of the name has long gone, all that can be seen from the public footpath is a small section of the moat and embankment. Meanwhile Hanley Swan is the quintessential English village with its duck pond, oak tree and a tastefully refurbished coaching inn beside the village green.

Getting There and Parking

Hanley Castle is located just over a mile and a half from Upton upon Severn on the B4211. It is only a short drive from Hanley Swan on the B4209. Hanley Swan lies on the crossroads of the B4209 and the B4208.

If arriving at the weekend or during the school holidays there is plenty of parking around the front of Hanley Castle High School. Otherwise, it might be better to park in Hanley Swan and begin the walk there.

When searching for bus timetables to the Hanley's it would appear there are quite a number until looking a little deeper to discover most serve Hanley Castle High

School for the school run. The 332 and 333 Worcester to Upton upon Severn provide two journeys to Hanley Castle on a Saturday and four during the week. The 363 Great Malvern to Tewkesbury which stops in Hanley Swan is just two journeys per day. The 373 Worcester to Upton upon Severn provides two trips per day via Hanley Swan. There is no Sunday service.

Maps

OS Explorer 190 Malvern Hills & Bredon Hill

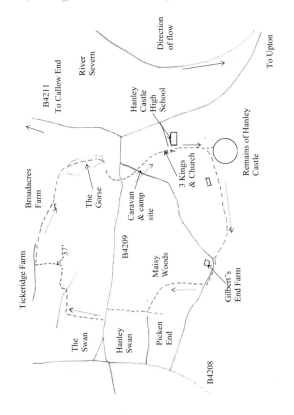

The Hanleys Map

A Little Slice of History

Devotees of P. G. Wodehouse might be interested to know that Hanley Castle High School was the fictional Market Snodsbury Grammar School which provided Bertie Wooster and Gussie Fink-Nottle's formative school days. P G Wodehouse's aunty Lucy was married to the reverend Edward Issac the vicar of St Mary's Church next door to the school. There is a small memorial plaque on the balustrade to the entrance of the Lechmere chapel. His gravestone is located in an overgrown section of the graveyard to the rear of the church. The school was founded in 1326 making it one of the oldest in the county.

St Mary's church is believed to have been built on the site of a Roman temple and extended during the Saxon period.

The Lechmere family
tombstones dated between
the ninth and eleventh
centuries are worth seeing.
The original church tower
was damaged during the
English Civil War and
replaced with the large
castellated brick tower in
1674.

The Hanleys' Village Society are quite a proactive
group and provide an informative website about the
village history, events and travel information. It is well
worth a look at www.hanleyswan.net

During one of my exploratory walks the good folk
of Hanley Swan had an open-garden event on the first
May Bank Holiday weekend which seemed to have
created a lot of interest from the number of people I
encountered.

Refreshments

The first of the two hostelries on this walk is the fifteenth-century Three Kings at Hanley Castle. At the time of writing the pub has not been decorated or refurbished probably since the 1950s (or possibly earlier). I could be doing it a disservice, but it certainly feels like this when you walk in. Whilst this may

appeal from an historical perspective, some folk may not be quite so keen imbibing in an authentic living museum. It may not be surprising to note that it is recorded in the Campaign for Real Ale's National Inventory of Historic Pub Interiors. The interesting pub sign of the three wise men has provided a range of stories from locals. However, in the seventeenth century the pub was owned by the three King brothers hence the name and play on wise men!

The Three Kings
Church End, Hanley
Castle WR8 0BL
Telephone 01684 592686

The second pub is
the very pleasant Swan
at Hanley Swan which
overlooks the village
green. It is a tastefully refurbished coaching house on
the route from the Welsh Hills to London. It still retains
a pub atmosphere whilst providing substantial dining
opportunities. Although I have not eaten there for many
years all the customers appear very happy with their
fare. Whilst I record, 'not dined', I have much enjoyed
their thrice fried chips after a Malvern Joggers club
night run. Needless to
say, the beer is excellent.

The Swan Worcester
Rd, Hanley Swan, WR8
0EA Telephone 01684
311870.

Along the Walk

If the weather has been inclement, it would be wise
to wear walking boots as a couple of the sections will be
muddy. Towards the end of the walk, it is likely there
will be cattle in the fields.

Heading Out for the Walk

Opposite the Hanley Castle High School car park
there is a delightful row of three Alms houses dating
from the 1600s. Head past the huge cedar of Lebanon
towards the Three Kings Inn.

Turn left and walk through the substantial wooden gate into the churchyard of St Mary's where the footpath goes around the church to the opposite end of this delightful churchyard to a rusty swing gate. Here the path leads down to the Pool Brook across a wooden bridge. However, our route is to turn left along the field boundary where not long after the path now drops down towards the Pool Brook. Cross over the stile and note the little sign for TROT which is an abbreviation of Toll Ride Off-road Trust.

Once over the brook, over to the left is the only visible sign of Hanley Castle, just an outline of a moat now covered in water lilies and a small section of the castle ramparts. This ancient man-made feature is in contrast to the rambling countryside which provides a strong feeling of peace and tranquillity. After enjoying your moment of contemplation or should we call it 'mindfulness'? return to the footpath walking away from the brook and slightly uphill. Pass through the swing gate and shortly after another swing gate where upon reaching level ground there is a great view of the Malvern Hills.

Whilst the footpath goes off to the right towards Lodge Farm, the OS map indicates a diagonal route across the field to the far corner where there is another swing gate. In fact, there appears to be more swing gates in and around the Hanley's than all of my other walks put together! The swing gate provides access into the next field where the path follows the field boundary. The path then continues across the middle of the next field towards Gilberts End Farm where it exits on the

bend opposite the farm buildings.

Turn left in the direction of the Malvern Hills and about four hundred metres further on, off to the right just before the speed restriction road sign the footpath sign points along a track towards paddocks. This must also be part of the TROT's route as one of their badges is nailed to a post.

Passing through the five-barred metal-gate the footpath continues straight on towards the trees between two basic wire fences. Upon reaching the line of trees our route is left over the stile and not across the ditch into the next field. The path runs alongside the ditch and trees to the next swing gate where

upon the trees provide an enveloping canopy overhead. Cross over a ditch into an enchanting clearing where two footpaths meet. A small sign indicates this is Maisy Woods.

Ignore the right-hand footpath. Continue straight on where a short distance further on, the outside world comes back into view. Cross over the farm track heading again towards the Malvern Hills. The path follows a wire fence to the next swing gate. The field boundary is now on the left of the footpath. There will be lambs and sheep or both in this field depending upon the time of year. The path continues towards the road and houses at Picken End. However, a transverse path crosses at this point so continue off to the right, heading towards the village where the path runs alongside garden fences. The path then

rather abruptly meets the B4209. Turn left towards the attractive Hanley Swan village green. There is an option here to deviate slightly and enjoy a refreshment break at the pleasant Swan Inn. Alternatively, the Post Office next to the crossing has a range of fresh food items. By my estimations it should have taken around an hour to have reached this point on the walk.

The non-refreshment route is to cross-over the road

and turn to the left where shortly the next footpath now follows an attractive track past Grassingdal Cottage and then a small orchard to the right. The path runs alongside the field boundary. On reaching the end of the field the path continues straight on crossing a small brook. Our route is to the right, keeping the brook and field boundary to the left. A short distance further on a swing gate leads to a basic bridge across the brook and onto some rough ground. The footpath sign points towards a small hill which is indicated as '37'm on the OS map. Unusually just ahead is a substantial track made of what looks to be concrete railway sleepers. On my first encounter with this track, I was wondering what on earth it was for? The cow pats might give the clue. Later that day I saw a very large herd of cows moving along it, I guess returning for their daily milking.

Back to our footpath. It appears to go diagonally across the field towards a swing gate just past the summit of this tiny hill. My research was carried out during the summer months and so full of crops. I took the option of walking along the concrete sleeper track a short distance and then joined the path running up alongside the field boundary. It was somewhat overgrown but not impassable. This little summit provides a fine view of the Malvern Hills. Our path now continues down-hill towards Tickeridge Farm. A footpath joins in from the right at a field boundary. Continue a little further where the footpath meets

the farm track. Turn
right heading away
from the Malvern Hills.
Although this should be
easier walking than the
footpath, there was on one
of my visits substantial
quantities of churned up
mud to contend with.

The muddy track passes farm buildings, old farm
machinery and a disused furnace. Ignore the next
two footpaths off to the right and continue along the
track. A track from Broadacres Farm joins from the
left. The route is slightly downhill in the direction of
the woods, towards two
metal five-barred gates.
Take the left-hand gate,
again with the TROT's
badge and cross over the
brook and into the woods.
The footpath nestles
between the high banks of
the adjoining fields and

climbs fairly steeply. The path opens out on reaching the small summit and carries on towards the B4211. Our route is off to the right through the woods which are indicated as 'The Gorse' on the OS map. This is a delightful woodland path which shortly meets a stile overlooking fields. The footpath waymarker points down the hill towards a wooden stile next to the field boundary. The adjoining picture shows a rather large herd of heifers very interested in Josh and myself!

The footpath continues along this wooded field boundary meeting the B4209. Cross-over the road where the footpath heads uphill and meets the minor road to Gilberts End Lane.

A small dogleg to the left and through the old rusty swing gate where the narrow footpath runs alongside the Maisy Cottage Caravan and Camping site. The last swing gate of the walk is encountered as the path traces the boundary of the Hanley Castle cricket green and the overgrown back garden of The Three Kings.

Waypoints

Hanley Castle High School car park: SO 83911 42036

Remains of Hanley Castle: SO 83843 41508

Towards Gilberts End Farm: SO 83270 41748

Track towards paddocks: SO 82543 42114

Left over the stile: SO 82508 42485

Houses at Picken End: SO 81637 42564

Meets the B4209: SO 81664 42918

Basic bridge across the brook: SO 81628 43498

37m: SO 81975 43696

Towards two metal five-barred gates: SO 83158 43591

The Gorse: SO 83430 42899

Meeting the B4209: SO 83358 42501

Maisy Cottage: SO 83604 42139

Notes and Observations from This Walk

Walk Six
Pershore and the River Avon

Summary

Pershore is a picturesque market town situated close to the River Avon in the Vale of Evesham. It is famous for its abbey founded in the seventh century and for the Pershore Plum Festival held each year in August. The impressive Abbey stands in a large park providing a peaceful backwater to the charming bustling market town where an abundance of early Georgian and Regency town houses flank much of Bridge Street, Broad Street and the High Street. Pershore also played a strategic role in the English Civil War.

The five-mile/8 km walk can commence from either the Harry Green Nature Reserve tucked away in Tiddesley Wood or just south of the town at Pershore Bridges. From Pershore Bridges car park the walk ventures along the banks of the sleepy River Avon and through Tiddesley Wood and then back into the charming town centre.

Getting There and Parking

Pershore is approximately ten miles south-east of Worcester and six miles west of Evesham. The A44 Oxford to Worcester Road bypasses Pershore close to the railway station. The town itself is served by the A4104 Upton Upon Severn and the B4084. The nearest motorway junctions are junction 7 of the M5 (South Worcester) or junction 1 of the M50.

Pershore does have a busy railway station on the main London to Hereford line operated by Great Western Railways however the station is just over a mile from the town centre.

Bus services are not too bad during the day with a number of buses such as the Number 51 and 52 serving the school traffic, the X50 providing an hourly service between Evesham and Worcester and after that there is an odd collection of infrequent buses and coaches operating once a day or on market days. From early evening onwards and on Sundays there are no bus services.

For those visiting the town centre free short stay parking is available in Broad Street and along the High Street. There are a number of pay and display car parks providing access to retail outlets and serving visitors to the Abbey. For this walk there is free parking at Pershore Bridges adjacent to the delightful Pershore Bridges Picnic Place located a quarter mile south of Pershore on the B4084 road to Evesham. Post code WR10 1AX, map reference SO 952 451. Also, at the opposite end of the walk out at the Harry Green Nature Reserve in Tiddesley Wood, there is a free car park operated by the Worcestershire

Wildlife Trust located half a mile west of Pershore on the Besford Bridge minor road. Post code WR10 2AD, map reference SO 929 462.

Maps

Ordnance Survey Explorer 190 Malvern Hills & Bredon Hill.

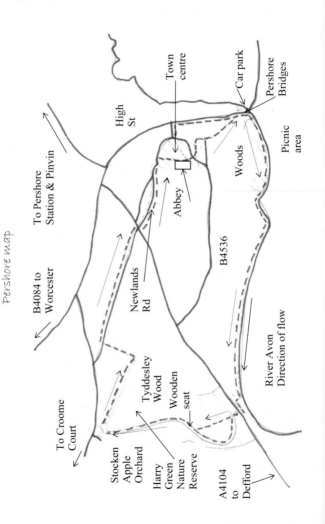

Pershore map

A Little Slice of History

The earliest precise date in the town's history is 681 when King Ethelred gave Oswald and Osric the land for the foundation of a religious house. The development of the abbey had a chequered history with the Benedictine monks being ejected, fires partially destroying the abbey in 1000, 1002 and in 1020 when there was even an earthquake! However, during this time there is a delightful story of Eadburga (also spelt Eadburgha) the granddaughter of Alfred The Great following the purchase by the Abbey of some of her relics. Following this, Pershore became a small-scale centre for pilgrimage. Eadburga until her death in 960 had been the abbess of a nunnery at Winchester. It is claimed that at the age of three she chose religious objects over jewels, gold and silver and this ensured she had a religious education. A blind man was apparently cured when he bathed his eyes with water in which Eadburga had washed her hands.

Unusually the town of Pershore had been part-owned and governed by Westminster Abbey until the Dissolution of the Monasteries. Henry VIII saw the nave and Lady Chapel together and all the monastic buildings were demolished.

Pershore was particularly vulnerable to the ravages of the Civil War as it commanded a strategic river-crossing on an important main road. Between 1642 and 1645 Parliamentary and Royalist troops plundered the town as they marched through. The river took its toll on both sides and in 1644 Charles's army demolished an arch of the bridge after escaping from Oxford and twenty soldiers along with a few officers as well as eighty countrymen were drowned. When a week later the Parliamentarians in pursuit of Charles entered Pershore a further sixty countrymen were found drowned.

The town grew up around its great abbey and close by a number of timber framed buildings dating back to medieval times are still in use.

In the eighteenth century the town developed as a staging post with the grand Angel Inn and Posting House now often referred to as just the Angel Inn. Broad Street was once the market place. However, the original market and fairs were held in the Abbey churchyard and this caused consternation with the local gentry. In 1830 an attempt was made by the leading citizens of the town to prevent a fair taking place by barricading the churchyard gates. The angry showmen and stallholders used an elephant and chain to pull down the barricade!

The development of Pershore as a market town is in part due to the abundance of local fertile land and an ability to grow a considerable range of fruits and vegetables. Nowadays, the most well-known crop is the Pershore Plum. The story goes that in 1833 George Crooks, the landlord of the Butcher's Arms, discovered the Egg Plum in Tiddesley Woods. Orchards were soon grown to exploit this crop and in 1890 a cross between plums produced the now famous Pershore Purple.

Pershore's agricultural heritage continues to this day with Pershore College of Horticulture, now known as Pershore College. It is a national centre for horticulture and is situated on a sixty-hectare site just past the two bridges on the Evesham Road.

Refreshments

If you get chance the Angel Inn is a treat, however there are a number of fine hostelries and cafés along and just off the High Street.

Along the Walk

The ground covered is a mixture of low-lying paths next to the River Avon, leafy and quite possibly muddy paths in Tiddesley Woods and conventional footpaths alongside the road into and through Pershore. There are a couple of stiles and swing gates to contend with. During the research phase for this walk the fields alongside the river had cows in them.

Heading Out for the Walk

If starting from the
Pershore Bridges free car
park take time to read
the local information
boards in the car park
and then head along the
old stone bridge where
one arch of the bridge was destroyed by Royalists
in 1664 fleeing to Worcester from Oliver Cromwell's
advancing forces. Note the more modern concrete anti-
tank defences which seem a little on the small side to
hold up an advancing force of Panza tanks. To access
the footpath alongside the river cross over the busy
main road. If starting this walk from the Harry Green
Nature Reserve in Tiddesley Wood continue from the

paragraph beginning with 'The broad main path through the woods leads'.

A multitude of walk route signs indicate the Millennium Way, Pershore Bridges Walk and Avon Valley Circular Walk are attached to the waypost pointing towards the steps leading down to the River Avon. Upon reaching the river path the Pershore Bridge picnic site can be observed across the river. The path follows the gently flowing River Avon downstream across an open field with views back to Pershore and the

Abbey. There is quite a substantial escarpment on the opposite side of the river as the path heads towards a small wood.

The River Avon and the neighbouring woods provide a tranquil setting along this section of the walk. Cross over the wooden bridge spanning a ditch and soon the view opens out over the fields towards the town. Across

the river there are distant views of Bredon Hill. The path can be a little muddy here alongside the river. During my visits there were cows grazing in the fields and swans enjoying the gentle flow of the Avon. After crossing the fourth and final wooden bridge over the field boundary ditches

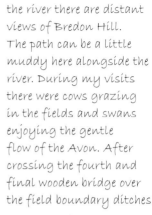

the footpath heads away
from the river a short
distance towards the busy
A4104. On reaching the
road follow the broad strip
of grass off to the left
where on the opposite side
there is an attractive large

sandstone coloured house. After approximately thirty
metres or so cross over the road to the footpath heading
uphill into Tyddesley Wood where the waypost indicates
the Two Bridges Circular Walk. Do note that the OS
map spells Tyddesley with a 'y' and the Worcestershire
Wildlife Trust spells it with an 'I'! When describing
the walk to some friends I rather mistakenly called it
Tiddly Wood!

After walking up the broad track for about one
hundred metres there are two options. Off to the right
there is a small potentially muddy path heading
uphill through the woods which meets up with the
track further on. This shortcut misses out the large
sweeping left-hand bend around the woods. Either way
the track climbs to the highest point in the woods where
kindly the Worcestershire Wildlife Trust have placed
a wooden seat. As with many of these Wildlife Parks
there are a multitude of paths to follow providing
exploring possibilities with very little chance of
getting lost. Ahead there are signs and red flags
denoting a military firing range in the south-west
corner of the woods.

The broad, main path through the woods leads
off to the right in a northerly direction and then
downhill towards Bow Brook providing a view of open

countryside. After crossing a stile, the footpath meets up with a perpendicular path running alongside the edge of the woods to the right. Where there also appears to be a cycle path just inside the fence of the woods. Over to the left of the footpath there is a substantial plum tree orchard. Continue to circumnavigate the woods. which

makes a further right-hand turning to a track, where over to the left there is an information board describing the Stocken Apple Orchard. The apples are used to make cider by the local horticultural college just outside Pershore on the Evesham Road. Turn to the right again following the edge of the woods where not long after the entrance from the Tyddesley Wood Worcestershire Wildlife Trust car park meets up from the left. Here there is an information board describing that in this ancient woodland the Pershore Yellow Egg Plum was cultivated.

Passing through a galvanised swing gate the path now goes slightly uphill and continues around the edge of the woods with open fields to the left and with the Abbey and town coming back into view. The

woodland boundary is off to the right. The footpath
turns to the left around a gated compound and follows
the field boundary. It then crosses a large field towards
civilisation in the form of Holloway Drive.

Follow the drive along the broad footpath towards the
town. On meeting the A41044 there are a number of
options depending on how busy or quiet one's preference
of this last section of the walk is to be. Opposite is New
Road which passes through a semi-industrial area
into the lower end of Newlands. Alternatively turn
left and a little further on the quieter more residential
Newlands Road leads into town. The Talbot hostelry
and Abbey Newlands fish bar are towards the Abbey
end of Newlands. Continue a little further along this
quiet backwater past a delightful black and white
timbered house to the
mini roundabout at the
junction of Abbey Road,
Church Row and the car
park opposite the Abbey
Park.

On reaching Abbey
Park the Abbey is indeed
an impressive structure.
However, it is immediately
apparent it has a strange
looking profile with
its huge buttresses. Of
course, one might guess
Henry VIII had something
to do with this during the
time of the dissolution of
the monasteries. He had

the nave destroyed. But good fortune has not followed the life of the Abbey. It has suffered several fires, an earthquake and the north transept collapsed in the middle 1600s. However, a number of historians describe it as one of the finest examples of Norman and Early English architecture in the country and is well worth a visit in a post-pandemic lockdown world.

The interior is rather spectacular. The ploughshare vaultings on the ceiling are very impressive. Arthur Mee in his 'Worcestershire' book describes: 'The great

array of vertical lines carries the eye to a vaulted roof which is the crowning glory of this builder's masterpiece, and is unsurpassed in any English church.' Maybe the vaulted ceiling accounts for the superb acoustics of the Abbey I rather enjoyed when listening to the Brighouse and Rastrick Brass Band many, many moons ago.

I have always found the Abbey warm and inviting with the helpful guides providing an historical perspective. On entering the Abbey, the Abbots Tomb (Edmund Hert 1456-79) and the crusader's tomb (probably

Sir William de Harley)
dominates the transept.
The rest of the tour of the
Abbey I shall leave to the
guides!

On leaving the Abbey
a delightfully peaceful
route to take is through the
Abbey Park and around
the children's playground
passing under an avenue
of oak trees which emerge
onto the Defford Road.

Alternatively, to
enjoy the hustle and
bustle of this pleasant
market town, head out
of the park behind the
Abbey onto Church Row
next to the White Horse
Hotel. Go left here along
Church Street past the
Town Council Visitor
Information Centre and
Library which emerges
onto the High Street. Or
continue along the side of
the Abbey boundary along
Church Row leading into
Broad Street which was
once the marketplace for

the town. Continue left passing Lloyds Bank to the
junction of Bridge Street. Opposite over to the left is the

Angel Inn and Posting House. Take a right along the attractive Bridge Street where 300 m or so further down on the opposite side of the road is Pershore's finest house, Perrott House at number 17 Bridge Street. Three storey, three bays built in 1760 for Judge Perrott a Baron of the Exchequer. It is believed Robert Adam, who designed the decoration at Croome Court designed the interior. Then continue along Bridge Street a ¼ mile or so to the two bridges car park.

Returning to the quieter route, on reaching the Defford Road there is an Abbey Park information board on the boundary wall and opposite a short dogleg to the right across the road to the Pershore and District Sports Club. The footpath goes around the sports ground and cricket pitch fence. After passing the cricket pitch don't turn left here as this goes back into town but follow the curvy brick wall to an attractive wrought iron fence. Here there are two footpaths one heading back to Bridge Street and the other straight on towards the water meadows. Cross over the end of the Nogains cul-de-sac onto a fairly rough path alongside allotments to the right and through an open stile onto the water meadows and back to the Pershore bridges.

Waypoints

Pershore Bridges car park: SO 95247 45079
Fourth and final wooden bridge: SO 93436 44902
Into Tyddesley Wood: SO 93300 44924

Towards Bow Brook: SO 92666 45343

Stocken Apple Orchard: SO 92644 46054

Pershore Yellow Egg Plum: SO 92935 45955

Around a gated compound: SO 93519 45720

Abbey Park: SO 94676 45845

Pershore and District Sports Club: SO 94839
45483

Nogains cul-de-sac: SO 95041 45335

Notes and Observations from This Walk

Walk Seven
Malvern Link to North Malvern

Summary

Although the Malvern area is famous for its breath-taking scenic walks, I have included just one in this volume. Another twelve walks in and around the Malvern Hills have been written by yours truly in the Pictorial Guide to the Malvern Hills series of four books which, I might add, provide exceptionally good value if all five (including Ledbury) are purchased through my website: www.malvernwalks.co.uk

I have undertaken this three-mile walk on a number of occasions particularly with large groups as it gives a 'taster' of the Malvern Hills without actually walking too far up any of them. Additionally, there are also plenty of historical points of interest to enhance this short experience of the Malverns. The text for this walk begins at Malvern Link railway station and finishes at the Nags Head which is across the Link Common from the station.

Getting There and Parking

There is plenty of free on street parking around the Nags Head, but not so when the pub is busy. Fifty-eight parking places are available at Malvern Link railway station for just £1 per day. There is also the North Malvern car park which is run by the Malvern Hills Trust and is expensive for a short stay at £4.50.

If arriving by train Malvern Link station is the starting point for this walk. The 44 Worcester to Malvern bus provides a frequent service along the Worcester Road passing the station, Link

Common and a stop just down from the Nags Head. There are even buses on Sundays!

Maps

OS Explorer 204. OS Landranger 150.

Malvern Map

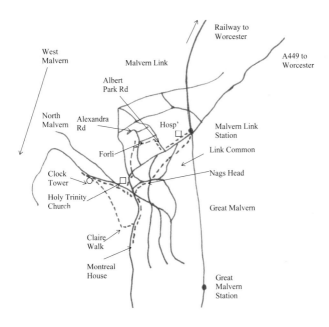

A Little Slice of History

Malvern Link station opened up for business in 1861 and provided a journey time to London of around six hours which was a substantial time saving from the two days by horse and carriage. Now in 2020, its two hours and thirty minutes. Although Great Malvern station provides a more direct access to the main town of Great Malvern it was the Malvern Link station that handled large volumes of visitors. The reason for this was due to Lady Emily Foley. As a benefactor of Great Malvern Station, a rich landowner and lady of influence she could not bear the thought of the day-trippers from the Black Country descending upon the genteel charm of Great Malvern and thus were, shall we say not encouraged to venture any further than Malvern Link.

The volume of day trippers was considerable. In 1861 the entire population of the Malvern area was exceeded by the 5000 visitors which would arrive each week. They were provided with entertainment befitting their status in life. A large hotel with ballroom was built where the 1960s flats and garages now reside on the platform 2 side of the station. The only evidence of this complex are the ornate black painted wrought iron gates partially hidden by the waiting room which provided the entrance to the hotel. Across the Worcester Road from the station the Link Common was also a key component in the entertainment programme where fetes, horse racing and balloon ascents attracted crowds of up to ten thousand in the 1860s.

Refreshments

The finish point of the walk is the Nags Head which is one of Malvern's finer hostelries. There is always a wide choice of beers and ciders, a couple of pleasant beer gardens and a restaurant.

Along the Walk

Underfoot it is a mixture of tarmac and stony paths. There is a steep flight of steps at the lower end of the Clare walk section which if ascending does increase the heart rate somewhat, otherwise it's a pleasant easy going walk.

Heading Out for the Walk

Commencing from Malvern Link station which underwent a well-earned facelift in 2014. Cross over to platform 2 and note the black painted wrought cast iron gates behind the waiting room. This is all that's left of a Gothic styled hotel and ballroom which served the influx of tourists in the 1860s. It is recorded that crowds of up to ten thousand would congregate on the common opposite the station enjoying fetes, balloon rides and horse racing. The house at the

end of platform 1 was the
station master's house.
It underwent substantial
restoration a few years
back and is now let as
a holiday destination,
available through
cottages.com.

Walk towards the
Worcester Road passing
through the pleasant
Malvern Community
Forest garden. Turn right
uphill along the Worcester
Road past the community
hospital. A little further
on note the rare Greek
styled fluted column
postbox. It is one of five
that still exist. There are
three in Malvern, one in
Solihull and the fifth has
been located in Australia
at the Old Telegraph
Station in Alice Springs.
They were made in 1857
and were designed by the
Post Office in conjunction
with the Government
Department of Science
and Art.

A little further up on
the opposite side of the

road the rather grand Temperance Drinking Fountain
is worth a visit. It was built in 1900 by members
and friends of the British Women's Temperance
Association. Around the tap it is inscribed with
'Whosoever will let him take of the water of life freely'.
Unfortunately, the water source is not from a spring
but is mains water. Continue heading uphill and turn
right into Albert Park Road away from the noisy
Worcester Road. This

is a pleasant suburb of
stylish Victorian villas
and modern dwellings.
Continue a short distance
and then turn left up
Somers Road and then
at the top, left onto
Alexandra Road. Note the
name 'Somers' originates
from Earl John Somers
Cocks who provided the
land for St Matthias's
Church in the Link. The
earldom became extinct
in 1882. The current
descendant of the Somers-
Cocks family is the Hon.
Mrs Hervey-Bathurst, daughter of the late Lord Somers
and resides at Eastnor Castle.

    A very short distance along Alexandra Road cross
over to Forli at number 37. On the stone pillar a small
brass plaque describes that Elgar lived here between
1889 and 1898. This peaceful suburb proved productive
for Elgar. He composed much of Caractacus and the

Enigma Variations alongside other works which expanded his local reputation into a national one.

Continue up the driveway where number 37 is the last house on the right. At this point the driveway meets Laburnham Walk. Turn left away from the house along this alleyway as it snugly sits between the gardens of houses on either side. Soon it meets the Worcester Road next to the Eversley newsagents where the owner prides himself on his extensive range of local beers. Turn right and head uphill to the junction of Newtown Road and the Worcester Road. On the right is the well-respected French bakery, Le Delice.

Opposite, across the junction the Holy Trinity church dominates the view towards Great Malvern along with its church hall. An option here is to cross over Newtown Road at the traffic lights and through the cast iron

gate alongside the church hall. A short dogleg leads into the churchyard where a number of paths circumnavigate the church and up onto the North Malvern Road. On reaching the road look to the left where there is an unusual thatched round house. Just a few paces down the road tucked into the side of the churchyard lies a tiny house, which when I first moved to Malvern was a public convenience.

Continue uphill where a short distance on the opposite side just past the junction with Lodge Drive are the remains of the Stocks Drinking Fountain constructed in 1895 by the Malvern Society for the Prevention of Cruelty to Animals. Behind the fountain are the stocks and whipping post. It is said that men

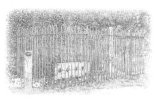

who had imbibed too much were carried up from the public houses for a twelve-hour penance in the stocks.

From the stocks there is a pleasant path running

parallel to the road or if wet, use the footpath leading up the North Malvern Road. Cross over the junction with the Hereford & Bromyard B4219 road and continue up into North Malvern. The path on the grassy bank comes to an end at the bus shelter. Opposite are a couple of retail outlets one being a cycle shop. A little further on a brown brick building now called Dixey Court was once the North Malvern School for Boys and opened in 1886. Continue uphill passing on the left the entrance to North Quarry car park. Before taking a look at the impressive clock tower ahead the former

Morris School for Girls is to the right. Both the clock tower and school were financed by Charles Morris. The school opened in 1838 and from 1942 to 1991 was the North Malvern Infants School. During one of my presentations to a local WI group a lady informed me that she had attended the school and had a story to tell. One morning during playtime the siren sounded from the quarry informing all that a blast was about to take place. Following the explosion, a large rock crashed onto the tiny playground miraculously missing all the children. From that day on, if the siren sounded during break time the children were immediately brought back into the school building.

Walk over to the Clock Tower which was built in 1843. The impressive building serves two purposes. The square structure behind the tower contains the water tanks creating a reservoir of water which in 1843 before the advent of mains water was the only source of water for the local inhabitants.

The clock tower is of course self-explanatory. However, note that the date on the circular stone reads 1901 some fifty-seven years after its construction. Charles Morris died in 1856 and by 1900 the tower needed repairing. The District Council undertook the renovation and extended the height of the tower and in doing so moved

the clock. In the hole left by the clock the circular inscription now resides.

Walk down the road passing on the right the Tank Quarry car park. If looking for a picnic spot, venture up the car park entrance and to the right above the car park is a pleasant grassy area with fine views, seats and a Geological Trail.

Ahead is the North Hill Quarry car park entrance. Keep to the right where a tiny footpath parallel to the car park provides an excursion to an information board describing the geology of this part of the hills. Keep to the path and through the trees you will see the remains of structures used in the quarry. Now head up the broad gravel path past the car park ticket machine.

After passing a house on the left, shortly after a path joins up from the left where there is a stone sign denoting the Alice Betteridge walk. Alice was a donkey lady possibly the last one to provide donkey rides taking folk up onto the hills. Head along Alice's path and through the trees.

Down below is Joyner's Common where you might just discern a footpath crossing the field, I did once scramble down the steep wooded slope to the footpath but it is not recommended!

At the next junction of the path take the lower one and head downhill, soon meeting an old flight of steps with the top section in a poor state of repair, over to the left there is a large radio mast. On reaching

the bottom of the steps a sign on the wall indicates Claire Walk. I am afraid Claire is a mystery to me. (If you find out please contact me on info@malvernwalks.co.uk). The steps are located at the entrance of a private driveway of numbers 59, 61 & 63 Worcester Road. Turn to the right in the direction of Great Malvern passing the carpet shop. Cross over the road to the fine looking white painted Montreal House. The blue plaque describes how Charles Darwin stayed here with his daughter Anne whilst being treated by a pioneer of the Malvern Water Cure, Dr James Manby Gully.

Now head down the Worcester Road on the final
short leg of this walk. Next to the bus stop there is an
old disused post box. It is painted green which originally
many years ago fooled me into believing it was a
very old post box which were originally painted green.
However, note the large GR, which of course indicates
George Rex of George the V fame as more commonly
referred to (he was the monarch from 1910 to 1936).

Passing the Malvern podiatry
centre Bank Street dips
down to the right. On the wall
of this Regency house the
blue plaque commemorates
Hugh Stuart Boyd who lived
here and taught Greek to
Elizabeth Barrett who later, of
course, was Elizabeth Barrett
Browning.

Continue down the
rather steep Bank Street
(Malvern has only three
'streets' and this is one of
them). Crossing Zetland
Road a little further down
is our final stop the popular
watering hole, The Nags
Head. But before availing
yourself of refreshments, on
the opposite side of the pub is
an interesting sign. When I
pose the question to my fellow
walkers, normally it's a
female who gets it right. It is

the sign for the Women's Institute. It would appear that the Malvern branch were one of the earliest groups in the country to form in 1924. During one of my reconnaissance walks I met a charming eighty-four-year-old lady who informed me that in its day the hall was quite a focal point of local entertainment. Now, it hardly looks big enough to swing a cat in it.

Waypoints

Malvern Link Railway Station: SO 78249 47477
Albert Park Road: SO 77917 47253
Alexandra Road: SO 77632 47363
Laburnham Walk: SO 77574 47341
Worcester Road: SO 77528 47048
Stocks and whipping post: SO 77467 46842
Clock Tower: SO 76989 47043
Alice Betteridge walk: SO 77231 46825
Claire walk: SO 77527 46414
Nags Head: SO 77674 46903

Notes and Observations from This Walk

Walk Eight
Powick Bridge to Worcester City Centre

Summary

The tiny River Teme and the mighty River Severn provide a very pleasant riverside walk into the centre of Worcester where there is an opportunity to explore this historic city. The first section of the walk beside the Teme and then the Severn up to the Diglis footbridge follows the Monarch's Way footpath. The footpath is alongside the riverbanks and can be a tad muddy if it has been raining, otherwise the rest of the walk is on metalled footpaths. As detailed in walk three, the River Severn is very prone to flooding which can render much of this walk impassable, so do check local weather reports if venturing from afar.

Industrial archaeology buffs should find this walk of interest and for train lovers there is a miniature railway to enjoy. Canal boat enthusiasts will enjoy

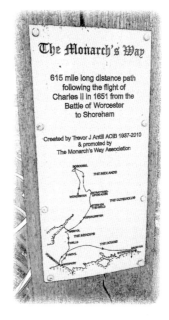

the Diglis Basin section of the walk with a myriad of narrow boats of all shapes and sizes moored up near the access point of the River Severn with the Worcester & Birmingham Canal. Once in Worcester there is, of course, an abundance of retail therapy to be had. Since Worcester was so embroiled in the English Civil War there are a number of historic sites of interest and, of course, the cathedral. All of which are referenced in the history section at the beginning of this book.

Getting There and Parking

There is a small free car park close to the old Powick bridge, plenty of on street parking on the industrial estate near the Diglis bridge and large pay and display car parks in Worcester near the Race Course and Technical College. For those arriving by train Worcester Foregate Street is a short walk from the River Severn. The bus station is even closer to the river, just follow the lie of the land down to the Severn. Worcester is quite a tiny city and once in the city centre there is little chance of losing your bearings.

Maps

OS Explorer 204 Worcester & Droitwich Spa

Powick to Worcester map

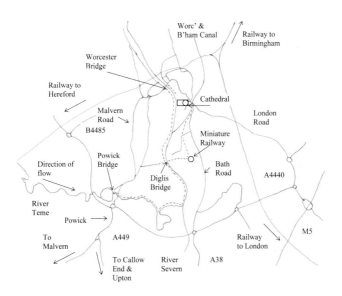

A Little Slice of History

Powick power station located next to the River Teme was originally a water mill. It was rebuilt in 1894 to become the world's first combined steam and hydro-electric power station. Close by is Powick old bridge a late mediaeval sandstone and brick-built structure. The importance of the bridge to gain access to Worcester meant that it saw action in 1642 with one of the first skirmishes of the English Civil War and later in 1651 at the Battle of Worcester where a section of the bridge was destroyed by the Royalists. Memorials commemorating these two battles and the Scottish soldiers who died at the Battle of Worcester are located on and next to the bridge. The fields on the Worcester

side of the Teme were the setting for the final battle of the English Civil War in 1651.

On approaching Worcester alongside the River Severn the Diglis Lock basin of the Worcester & Birmingham Canal provides a good example of Victorian water engineering. A little further on the mid-eighteenth-century Diglis House Hotel was originally the home of Edward Leader Williams, the chief engineer of the Severn Navigation Commission. He was a keen amateur artist and was friendly with

John Constable. His son Benjamin accompanied his father on sketching trips and this influence led to Benjamin studying at the Royal Academy of Arts. His landscape paintings soon began to sell all over the world, including a purchase by William Gladstone. Edward, the second eldest son became the chief engineer of the Manchester Ship Canal and was knighted for his work on the canal.

The Commandery is a substantial black and white timbered Grade 1 listed building next to the canal and main thoroughfare into the city. It was the Royalist headquarters during the final battle of Worcester.

Refreshments

A huge choice in Worcester of course and en route the large Manor Farm eatery on the Malvern Road, WR2 4BS, which is a stone's throw from Powick Bridge. The Cathedral Cloister Cafe, Clockwatchers in Mealcheapen Street in the centre of the city, the Worcester Chippy close to Deansway and the Café Afloat in Diglis Basin all come highly recommended. Additionally, for something completely different and not commonly known the Old Palace more often referred to as the Bishops Palace on Deansway between the cathedral and technical college. I have had lunch here rubbing shoulders with a Bishop or other members of the clergy at a very reasonable cost served by delightful ladies who are it seems very pleased to see new diners at their tables.

Along the Walk

It is likely there will be sheep in the fields next to the River Teme.

Heading Out for the Walk

The small parking area near Powick power station backs onto a section of the rail track which I am guessing must have provided coal to fire the power station. The information board describes the history of the site from medieval water mill to hydro-

electric power station. Turning in the direction of the tall chimney of the refurbished power station the old road leads towards the sandstone bridge. On the left next to the swing gate is a large carved stone describing the Scottish involvement in the English Civil War.

Although the footpath for our route leads off towards the current road bridge take the opportunity to walk onto the old bridge where you will obtain a good view of the refurbished

power station and run off from the power station into the River Teme. Looking away from the power station the new, rather impressive footbridge over the link road was completed in 2021. Now head back to the footpath and into the field towards the new road bridge. Over to the left in the middle of the field looks like an interesting object. Don't bother, it's

only a sewer outlet! Continue towards the bridge, a sign not only in English but in Polish informs of 'no fishing'. The path goes under the bridge and then diagonally left across the middle of the field, or alternatively follow the steep bank of the River Teme. If you are new to the area this floodplain is often to be found under many feet of water during the winter months.

Although there is only the one sign just inside the field to indicate you are walking on history, this is the very location of the battlefield which ended the English Civil War.

The path meets up again with the river where if the gate is closed cross over the stile. There are cows sometimes in these fields. The path follows the bank of the Teme to a point where fifty metres or so over to the left the same footpath heads off towards Worcester. There is at this point a large ox-bow section of the river. Choose whether to go around the ox-bow where a little further on the opposite bank of the river is an unusual location for a property (Temeside Cottage) built in the middle of an established flood plain. If taking the

short cut follow the Teme to where it meets its big brother the River Severn. Now continue along the bank of the Severn where a short distance further on the Worcester city boundary sign is passed.

Continue towards the city where the cathedral spire provides a convenient marker ahead. A little further on over to the left the golf driving range with its rusty target cars comes into view. The path continues on the high riverbank towards the relatively new Diglis Bridge built in 2010.

Cross over the springy suspension bridge. Continue straight on

with the foot and cycle
path sign indicating the
city centre immediately
left the Severn Way to
the right and straight
on (our route) Withy
Bed Way, St Peter's. All
of these paths are well
used by commuters and
tourists alike. A shorter
route if time is short
would be left alongside
the river, however a slight
detour for the model train
buffs reading this text.
The path heads away from
the river where over to
the left is an industrial
estate. Continue across
the flood plain towards
the higher ground ahead
where the Bath Road

makes its way into the city centre. A little further
on over to the right is a compact miniature railway
track complete with tunnels, engine sheds, etc. It is

run only at weekends and Bank Holidays, see the Worcester and District Model Engineers Facebook page for further details. Our route towards the city is now left either across the playing fields or follow the path which circumnavigates the field towards an access road and pile of standing stones.

The path out of the park crosses an access road towards the relatively new Diglis housing development. Follow the new road through a street of town houses towards the basin of the Worcester & Birmingham canal. This is a pretty area where old meets new. Take advantage of the delightful canal boat café and then head off to the right where the large basins on both sides provide long-term moorings for this little Venice. Again, if time is

short go left towards the Severn and continue along the riverside path into Worcester.

Go left past the chandlers following the path around the left-hand basin meeting the Anchor pub on the right. A little further on the path now follows the canal where the opposite bank once contained the Worcester Porcelain factory which is now quite densely packed with town houses. Watch out for the mooring posts otherwise you might find yourself in the canal. A little further on the canal meets the road bridge and a tiny lock gate. Take the path away from the canal at the lock gate which brings you alongside The Commandery.

On reaching the main road, turn right towards the city over the bridge and alongside a parade of shops. On reaching the

crossroads look over to the opposite side where there are a few small sections of the old City Wall. Cross over towards the cathedral and straight on along Edgar Street.

College Green is through the impressive arch. This is a little oasis from the busy city. The first turning towards and into the cathedral leads to the Cloisters Café. There is plenty to see in the cathedral and even a small bookshop selling copies of this book.

Exit through the main entrance on the city side of the cathedral to further explore the city or alternatively back onto College Green and down towards the river (continues after the next paragraph). If not wishing or not able to enter the cathedral, the route into the city is back through the archway and immediately left up a couple of steps into the

cobbled Edgar Street. Further
along on the right is a plaque to
Elgar. Meeting the main road turn
to left into Elgar Square. It is a
real shame that the town planners
many moons ago cut off the
cathedral from the city with this
busy thoroughfare. This would be
a good time to avail oneself of the
attractions of the city.

However, keeping to
the walk continue along
Deansway with the college
buildings to the left and
opposite the fine watering
hole The Plough next to
the former fire station
and following it the police
station. Following the
St Andrews building

of the college there is a turning down to the left to the Copenhagen Street car park. Unfortunately, there is no statue of a little mermaid, but there is a picnic area next to Browns with (if they are working) a timed set of water spouts which are great fun for young children to enjoy.

If you are intending to reach the river via College Green go down the flight of steps through the stone archway and note the flood markers set high on the walls indicating the height of floods over the past three hundred years. Here on Sundays, there is a ferry across the river. Turn right towards the Worcester Bridge, in fact the only road bridge spanning the Severn for many a mile. The waterside promenade is often quite busy with locals and tourists alike.

Following the cathedral is the Old Palace where on

the riverbank is the Swan Statue, then the Technical College which is architecturally quite out of keeping. The stone cladding was meant to mellow with age and blend in with the cathedral and palace. What do you think, has it worked? I spent eleven years working at the college which was then known as Worcester College of Technology. The path continues past the city centre car park and to the aforementioned fountains, possibly the only waterfront attraction the city council has undertaken. With the fountains operational and the café in full swing this is a delightful recreational area. The path leads past Browns restaurant and up to the Worcester Bridge where if folk lore is correct one can legally shoot a Welshman with an arrow! I don't advise trying it out on my say so!

Standing on Worcester Bridge provides fine views and iconic photo opportunities. There are no pedestrian crossing points on the Worcester side of the bridge, so if attempting to head upstream towards the railway viaduct and racecourse. Cross the single lane Bridge Street and go along North Quay passing The Rectifying House and Severn View Hotel. Here it is best to cross over the two lanes towards the river.

However, the route for this walk is to cross over the bridge towards the Premier Inn and Worcester Cricket Ground. Follow the path down to the left alongside the riverbank past the car park and boathouse. Opposite there are photo worthy views of the Bishops Palace and the cathedral. Here is the other side of the inexpensive

ferry service. Part of the cricket ground can be seen off to the right of the towpath. Continue along this pleasant leafy path through the area known as Chapter Meadows and towards the weir where at the time of writing a char leap was being constructed.

The weir spans across to Diglis Island where the lock is located on the opposite bank and then a little further on the Diglis Bridge comes into view. Just before the bridge there is a right-hand turning indicated by the blue sign pointing away from the river leading up towards an industrial estate. The path joins Weir Lane which is the main entrance and exit to the estate. If you have brought your swimming gear Lower Wick swimming

pool is over to the left alongside the golf driving range that was mentioned earlier. Recently a trendy coffee and doughnut shop has opened up in an industrial unit over to the left.

Continue along Weir Lane and on meeting the main road (Bromwich Road) turn left away from Worcester. Go along this busy arterial road towards the roundabout where opposite there is a small M&S store as part of the BP garage. Go straight over towards the large Manor Farm eatery which has over the years changed its name at least three times to my recollection.

There is a traffic island a little further on where its best to cross over the road (now the Malvern Road). A hundred metres or so Old Road returns to the lofty chimney stack of the Powick Power Station, thus concluding a delightful walk into Worcester.

Waypoints

Powick power station: SO 83538 52571
Ox-bow: SO 84502 52049
Worcester city boundary sign: SO 85011 52250
Diglis Bridge: SO 84694 53120
Miniature railway track: SO 85195 53280
Canal boat café: SO 84994 53877
The Commandery: SO 85253 54410
Cloisters Café: SO 85000 54469
Worcester Bridge: SO 84645 54789

Notes and Observations from This Walk

Helpers

My thanks go to Colin Soley, Brian and Mary Bade, Geoffrey Aston, Joshua Flint, Natasha Flint, Sharon Flint, and Nigel Lightfoot for helping to undertake and check the walks. Nigel also provided photographs for the Pershore and Bredon Hill Walks.

Bibliography

Barrett, Phillip & Wilson, Marshall. The Book of Pershore. 1980 Barracuda Books Ltd.

Cox, Benjamin. The Book of Evesham. 1977. Barracuda Books Ltd.

David & Charles Touring Companion. Worcester, The Malverns & surrounding area. 1990. David & Charles Newton Abbot.

Defoe, Daniel. A Tour Through the Whole Island of Great Britain. First Published in 1724-26. This edition 1971. Chivers-Penguin.

Freeman, Barry. Worcestershire. 1996 Shire Publications Ltd

Grundy, Michael. Elgar's Beloved Country

Hallow History Group. Hallow Farms and Mills Past and Present. 2013. Hallow History Group.

Houghton, Colin & Darien-Jones, Nick. Broadway Pictorial. 2004. Darien-Jones Publishing

Hurle, Pamela. Hanley Castle Heart of Malvern Chase. 1978. Phillimore & Co. Ltd

Long, Peter. The Hidden Places of Herefordshire, Worcestershire & Shropshire. 1999.Travel Publishing

Mee, Authur. The Kings England Worcestershire The Garden in the Hills. 1938. Hodder and Stoughton

Pevsner, Nikolaus. The Buildings of England Worcestershire. 1968 Penguin Books

Smith, Brian S. A History of Malvern. 1978. Alan

Sutton & The Malvern Bookshop

Taylor, Christopher. Roads & Tracks of Britain. 1979. J.M. Dent & Sons Ltd

Westwood, Brett. Worcestershire Countryside. Minton and Minton

Worcestershire Federation of Women's Institutes. The Worcestershire Village Book. 1988. Countryside Books, Newbury and the WFWI, Worcester

About the Author

Carl Flint has published to date five Pictorial Guides illustrating walks in and around the Malvern Hills and Ledbury. Following his semi-retirement from the world of education there has been more opportunity for him to venture further afield into the Worcestershire countryside and detail a collection of new walks for these three volumes.

Carl started off his career in the music electronics industry where he was fortunate to experience the exciting and creative atmosphere of music and film studios. Standing on the plywood remains of Luke Skywalkers transporter from the first Star Wars film at Elstree or listening to The Who rehearse for their album 'Who are You' were seminal experiences.

The travel bug developed whilst engaged in studying firstly for a HND and then a Degree. The first trip to India was inspired by watching a slide show of a trip from London to Katmandu by road whilst in Amsterdam staying with friends. This moment is set in time as people who heard us speaking English in bars later that evening told us we were at war with Argentina!

The trip to India, Thailand and Malaysia the following year firmly set the exploration juices flowing and it was not by coincidence with the prospect of the long summer holidays that Carl's second career in teaching was born. Over the years following, further extended trips to India, Nepal and Bhutan were undertaken. Before the advent of mobile phone apps the only realistic way to plan your journey and then explore the country was through the amazingly informative Lonely Planet Guides. These guides also subconsciously through their structure and detail made a lasting impression which to some extent is reflected in the authors Pictorial Guides. The first travel writing-if you can call it that, were updates sent to the Lonely Planet publisher. The feedback from seeing your name in print as a contributor was rewarding.

Getting married and having children did not stop the travelling just the frequency and length of stay were reduced. Fortunately, my children have experienced the far-flung countries of Singapore, New Zealand, Dubai, India, Sri Lanka, Cambodia and Vietnam.

Teaching posts in Hampton Hill and Twickenham led Carl into Further Education. As a relatively 'young buck' at the beginning of the 1992 Further Education reforms this meant that a move into management ensured. First at department level, then faculty and finally after five years in Colwyn Bay a Vice Principal's post in Worcester.

The book writing career began following a senior leadership development programme where Carl's tutor expressed a very positive wish to read his next essay. Following the programme and buoyed up by praise Carl went to the local Waterstones and sought out books about walks in his home town of Malvern. With only one book on the shelves, Carl decided he could do better and self-published the first Pictorial Guide to the Malvern Hills in 2010.

At about this time the halcyon days of the Further Education sector began its terminal decline after Government cut backs followed by even more draconian cut backs broke the back of this once inspiring and 'life changing' sector of our education system. The book writing became a stress reliever, undertaking the walks and sitting down researching was an antidote to the redundancies taking place it seemed almost every month.

Following his own redundancy in 2012 Carl was fortunate to be involved in writing an academic paper on scholarly activity and undertook a Webmaster role for the higher education organisation the Mixed Economy Group. Then followed two periods of teaching in local secondary schools. An opportunity arose at the Royal College of Radiologists as a Lay Member for its Continuing Professional Development Committee which in turn led to lay roles with the Royal College of Physicians, which is possibly Carl's fourth or is it fifth career to date?

So, there is still life left in the old goat as he treks out to record walks in the furthest corners of the Worcestershire Countryside, he hopes you will enjoy the walks as much as he does!

Titles Available in the 'Pictorial Guides'

A Pictorial Guide to the Malvern Hills.
Book 1: North Malvern, West Malvern and
Malvern Link.
Published July 2010

A Pictorial Guide to the Malvern Hills.
Book 2: Great Malvern
Published 2010, Republished 2018

A Pictorial Guide to the Malvern Hills.
Book 3: Malvern Wells, Welland, Little
Malvern, British Camp, Castlemorton Common,
Hollybed Common and Whiteleaved Oak.
Published July 2012

A Pictorial Guide to the Malvern Hills. Book
4: The Royal Well, Colwall and Alfrick Pound
returning to the Dingle in West Malvern.
Published July 2014

Walks in and Around Ledbury:
A Pictorial Guide to Ledbury. Town Centre
Heritage Walk, A Brief History of Transport
in Ledbury and Ledbury to Eastnor Castle.
Published June 2017

Index